ANALYSIS OF MEDIA AND COMMUNICATION TRENDS

ANALYSIS OF MEDIA AND COMMUNICATION TRENDS

Editor

Prof. Ramesh Chandra

ISHA

ISBN : 978-81-8205-051-8

Published, 2018

Published by

Isha Books
D-69, New Gupta Colony,
Near DDA Market
Delhi – 110009
Ph.: +91-9212142040

Contents

Preface

The advent of digital communication technologies have produced a plethora of innovative interactive multimedia services and created a new distribution platform for audio and visual content and information. They have broughtout profound changes in how global citizens obtain news and feature programming, as well as how we communicate among ourselves and contribute to the emerging decentralized, many-to-many media system.

The mass media including television, radio, press, cinema, etc., are able to reach thousands/millions of receivers instantaneously through many sense modalities. They constitute the backbone of democracy. They identify problems in our society and serve as a medium for deliberation. They are also the watchdogs that we rely on for uncovering errors and wrongdoings by those who have power. It is therefore reasonable to require that the media perform to certain standards with respect to these functions, and our democratic society rests on the assumption that they do.

Today, the mass media are accepted as powerful forces in the process through which we come to know ourselves and one another. They function both as a forum in which issues are debated and as the storytellers that carry our beliefs across time and space. Through these roles, the media are central to the creation and maintenance of both our dominant culture and our various bounded cultures. This cultural orientation toward mass communication and the media places much responsibility on media consumers. In the past, people were considered either victims of media influence or impervious to it. The cultural orientation asserts that audience members are as much a part of the mass communication process as are the media technologies and industries. As important agents in the creation and maintenance of their own culture, audience members have an obligation not only to participate in the process of mass communication but also to participate actively, appropriately, and effectively.

Developments in the field of mass media and communication are elaboratively described in this book. The role and responsibilities of mass media in society are also discussed. Students, teachers, journalists, administrators and policy-planners will find this of utmost use.

Editor

1

Theories of Mass Communication

Mass media channels typically mean TV, Radio, Press, Cinema, etc. Here the message is able to reach thousands/millions of receivers instantaneously through many sense modalities. Mass media is called as the 'fourth estate' of democracy—a source of information, independent of the government. It prevents disproportionate power in the hands of a few, alone.

Some of the major theories of mass communication are described in this chapter.

Defleur and Rokeach's Dependency Theory of Mass Media Change

According to this theory, the potential of the media to bring about change would increase when there is instability in society. The uniqueness of the delivery system can also be the bases of change. The audience response in the model implies that feedback also has potential for change. So, the audience, media and society co-exist in a tripartite manner, in every society and jointly become the change agents.

Gozzi's Theory of Two Kinds of Mass Media Cultures

Gozzi identified two kinds of cultures in terms of mass media. The High context culture and the Low context culture. (HCC and LCC). Context refers to the implicit rules regarding how people handle information and relate to it. The mass media effects in terms of these two cultures is distinct and different.

High context culture (HCC)

1. The media context is distant in providing the context for describing the world.
2. Newer symbols and information are provided by the society to handle and interpret those com-ing from the media.
3. Media opinions and values do get countered by the interpersonal effects and networking of people.
4. Media representations are viewed as removed from reality.
5. Media influences are lesser.

Low context culture (LCC)

1. The media context is very close for des-cribing the world.
2. Newer symbols are provided by the mass media to fill in the con-cepts of social reality.
3. Media creates opinions and values that the majority silently, accepts.
4. Media creations are seen as very close to reality.
5. Media influences are higher.

The media effects in these to types of cultural contexts very. These have significant bearing on communication and its effects.

Theories Deal with the Content and Impact of Media

on Society

The four theories of the press presented by Siebert, Peterson and Schramm are:

1. *Authoritarian theory*

This theory talks about the role of communication in authoritarian countries. Here the rulers control the masses with the power they hold. The press is not free in such societies. There is censorship and tight control over the media.

2. *Libertarian Theory*

According to this theory the government has no right to control the press. The freedom to publish should rest with the media. The concept of liberty dominates this theory.

3. *Social Responsibility Theory*

According to this theory the media should be free but at the same time be socially responsible. The social responsibilities of the media include informing the public correctly about events and mould public opinion on every issue in a fair manner. This theory implies that the media has to combine responsibility with freedom on it's own accord, in keeping with the public good.

4.*Soviet Communist Theory*

According to this theory the media is part of the government and should be a voice of the government. So the media's role is to further the aims of the govern-ment. So independence of the media is not seen as necessary. After the second world war and the formation of the United Nations and other international bodies two more theories of media were formulated. These were in keeping with the needs of the new emerging independence that many countries obtained from their rulers.

McQuail's Theories of Mass Media

McQuail et al. proposed two theories of mass media.

1.Development Media Theory

The development media theory is specially relevant to countries like India which won independence from its colonisers in the late 1940s. According to this theory, the role of the media in general is to contribute towards the develop-ment of the country. This is the concept of development journalism. Media should be utilised for the development of the nation according to this theory. This is an important role that the media has to fulfil. Information and communication that serves the interests of growth and development should become a priority for the media, according to this perspective.

2.Democratic Participant Theory

According to this view the media and the people should jointly participate in the development of the country. This theory also values the democratic participation of the two in the progress of the nation. Both the people and the media should be free for participation in the country's progress.

Social Diffusion Theory

This theroy was proposed by Everett M Rogers. According to

this theory the spread of ideas in any community goes through several phases before being accepted or rejected. These stages are:

1. *Knowledge*: Gaining awareness about an issue.
2. *Persuasion*: The idea or issue is evaluated and appropriate attitudes towards it are developed.
3. *Decision*: On the basis of the evaluations made, the idea is either adopted or rejected.
4. *Confirmation*: Here the consequences of the decision are also reserved. The final acceptance or rejection takes place in this phase. Change occurs once the idea is accepted.

These steps appear to be suitable as an explanation for societies where ideas are suggested from outside of a given society rather than for those situations where the group or society itself throws up an idea on the basis of which, change should occur.

Social Learning Theory

This theory was propounded by Bandura Ross and Ross. According to them people learn social attitude and behaviours from the images, characterisations etc., presented by the media. This implies that we learn by observation and that media is a powerful communicator or teacher. TV is seen as a potent source of influence because of its visual capacity. Bandura clearly sees antisocial/aggressive behaviours to be largely learnt from portrayals on TV and Cinema. He calls these models for imitation. Mass media provides a huge context for social learning, according to this theory.

Media Cultivation Theory

This theory was proposed by Gerbner. It indicates that TV and Cinema suggest what reality is like through the portrayals of people and other images. For example by viewing TV or Cinema one gets to realise that violence is part of life or that marital infidelity is widespread. The greater the hours spent on watching TV; the greater the acceptance of reality as seen on the screen. Gerbner described 4 hours of TV viewing as light watchers while above 4 hours viewing gets to be categorised as heavy watchers.

Aggression Stimulation Theory

This is based on the formulations of Berkowitz. According to him the inmate tendency to aggress in an individual is bound to increase under certain conditions.

1. Viewing violence in the media.
2. Perceiving it as fair or appropriate
3. Seeing the similarity between the violence depicted by the media and the situation he/she is placed. For example one sees the hero bash up those who thwart his attempts. An individual who finds that his goals are being obstructed by others may engage in aggression as he has viewed similar behaviour in the media. He believes that aggression is an appropriate response to blocking goal attitudes. This tendency to aggress can be reduced if people are made to perceive that there is no connection between the aggression portrayed on the screen and the real-life situations in which people are placed. For example, people should be made to understand that the TV or Cinema is only a make-believe presentation. The superman who can take on several people all at the same time is a screen hero and that this does not apply to people in real-life.

Symbolic Catharsis Theory

The Symbolic Catharsis Theory was advanced by Feshbach. The main theme of his theory is that viewing violence in the media has a cathartic effect on the individual. By watching aggression and by identifying with the aggressor; the viewer can satisfy his/her own personal tendencies for violence or aggression. There prevents their actually engaging in aggression in their lives. There is an indirect psychological release of pent up feelings of aggression. This form of 'letting off steam' is believed to be a way of aggression prevention in real-life.

Modelling and Expectancy Value Theory

This theory was proposed by Fishbein. According to this theory people identify with the portrayals on TV and cinema, provided there are rewards for displaying similar behaviours or attitudes, in ones personal life. The motivations for engaging in similar behaviours arise from two factors:

1. Personal rewards or gains.
2. Social approval for engaging in similar actions.

If these are met then media portrayals tend to be significant in influencing behaviours.

Need Gratification Theory

This theory was put forward by Katz et al. They proposed that people satisfy their different personal/social needs from media depictions. There are 5 basic needs in individuals. They are:

1. *Cognitive needs*: Refer to the needs for being informed, stimulated, being aware etc.

2. *Psychological needs*: Refer to the needs for self-orientation, understanding etc., in terms of issues and events around us.
3. *Integrative needs*: Refer to the way in which people want to make sense about their environment and relate to people events etc. This is the need to understand and interpret things, by confirming, evaluating etc.
4. *Family needs*: These are based on the need for security, belongingness, etc., in individuals.
5. *Tension release or escape needs*: People have a big need to avoid unpleasantness or release their anger or frustrations.

TV or Cinema caters to all of these needs in one form or another. Depending on the dominant need of a given individual at a particular point of time he/she could use the different media communications to gratify his/her personal need states. Thus mass communication has need gratification as an essential component in its presentations, according to Katz's theory.

McLuhan's Theory of Communication

According to this theory Media itself is a compelling force regardless of the messages involved. Media has the power to alter sensory organisation and thought and thereby alter, society, eventually. Media can alter patterns of perceptions. Media is seen as an extension of human abilities and senses. Media has jolted man out of his cohesive tribal existence, believes McLuhan. Media has 'retribalised' man in a new way.

McLuhan also described media as being hot or cool. A hot medium (print, radio, film, photography) is one that extends a single sense with high definition that is a complete filling in of data, by the medium.

Hot media are low in participation by the audience. In a cool medium the audience is an active constituent of the viewing or listening experience. TV is a cool medium because it is visually low on data thus ensuring a lot of audience involvement.

McLuhan's theory is criticised on the grounds that he chooses to ignore the content of mass communication while focusing on the medium itself.

Semantic Theories of Communication

There are five theories that identify different functions of mass communication.

1. *Hobby*: Radio and television are seen by many as extremely popular and even addictive. To this extent, one function that this form of mass communication satisfies, is that of being a hobby or pastime.
2. *Journalism:* The need to be informed or to become aware is another function that mass communication carries out.
3. *Social reform*: The notion of media being used an agent of social change is implied in this function. New values and orientations can be projected by the mass media, to foster change. For example campaigns against dowry, bribes, untouchability etc.
4. *Sense extension*: Radio, TV, Cinema etc., arouse strong emotional reactions among people who listen or watch. To this extent these mass media communications have a role to play in terms of extending ones sensory characteristics, further and thereby engaging them.
5. *Play:* The play function of mass media refers to the fact

that it has become a part of the ordinary lives of people. Mass media can be viewed as a component of the common culture of everyday living. To this extent it is like play or fun to most listeners/viewers. This explains why many people are so keen on viewing their favourite programmes by setting aside time and rearranging their schedules.

Selective Attention/Perception and Retention Theory

This theory is based on the psychological processing of stimuli. The concepts of attention/perception and retention need to be clarified. This theory was proposed by Book et al.

Selective attention: This implies giving priority to a particular sensory message. This is the first stage of perception. We are surrounded by sights, sounds, colours, smells tastes and touch sensation. Which are we aware of? We select from the different inputs. This is selective attention. Selectivity is necessary for reducing the multiplicity of stimuli into a few. A few stimuli that are relevant or significant could be attended to better. This is not only important for survival but also for orienting oneself properly to the task on hand. The features of attention are:

1. It is selective
2. It can be divided
3. One can get habituated
4. It can be oriented
5. There can be lapses

All these factors determine selective attention.

Perception: This is the mental process of organising sensations into meaningful patterns. Perceptions are based on certain categorisations of experiences. These are determined by two factors.

1. Structural factors (these are present in the stimulus):
   a. Size
   b. Intensity
   c. Frequency
   d. Novelty
   e. Contrast
   f. Change
2. Functional factors (these are present in the individual):
   a. Motives
   b. Interests
   c. Needs
   d. Set or expectancies
   e. Familiarity/strangeness
   f. Emotions.

These two factors combine to determine whether a given stimulus is perceived or not. This refers to the selectivity of perception.

Retention: This refers to the storing or holding of information in memory.

Thus the three processes of selective attention, perception and retention proceed on the basis of stimulus and individual factors. This has big implications for mass communication in terms of how materials are received, perceived and retained. On the basis of these would rest the extent of influence. Such a conceptualisation is known as the individual differences perspective. This theory describes audiences in terms of learning, using a stimulus-response notion. Here, there is no such thing as a uniform audience. So mass media communi-cation affects each individual audience member differently in keeping with that individual's personal/psychological make up.

Hypodermic Needle Theory

The 20th century has been described as the age of mass-communication revolution. Mass media came up in a big way and its influence on people was very powerful. This was recognised for the first time. Scholars and researchers in the area came to realise that mass communication had a far reaching and pervasive effect on the audience. The messages were directed, pointed and extremely influential. This influence was described as the 'magic bullet theory' of communication. This implied that the mass media messages have a magical spell on the audiences. Further, the messages were presented in a capsule form and therefore have a bullet like piercing capability. Due to its capacity to be inserted at a given point but be able to bring about a change in the entire system or society; this theory also came to be known as the 'hypodermic needle theory' of mass communication. The main thrust of this theory is its pointed source of entry; but the overwhelming impact it comes to have later, on the entire system.

Theory of Limited Effects Model

According to this theory the impact of mass communication is limited in terms of creating public opinion. To begin with, not all segments of a society are addressed equally by any mass media message. Also, other societal influences such as culture, values, family, education, historical background, folklore, legends etc., also have a strong influence on people and their thought processes. Therefore the impact of mass communication is believed to be limited.

Two-step Flow Theory

Katz proposed the two-step flow theory of mass communication. He indicated that mass-media messages do not reach the audience, directly. It first goes to the opinion leaders and then in the second step goes to the audience through these power sources. The main concept behind this theory is that opinion leaders receive the mass media messages first and then in turn, the leaders pass on the messages to the people. Implied in this theory is the understanding that some amount of filtering of messages take place in step 1. This means that the opinion leaders allow certain messages to reach the audience while others are withheld. Therefore opinion leaders are the opinion makers. Their influence is more powerful than those of the mass communication messages, by themselves. Advertisers, politicians and others utilise this notion to their advantage, most pointedly. For example the use of sports personalities to sell or convey important messages to influence the audience. This theory is criticised on the ground that mass media involves more than merely a two-step process. There are a complex nexus of influences. There is always a time lag between the communication of the message and the receivers response. The respondent accepts the media message in terms of many factors. Education, training, attitude, orientation etc., are all significant determinants in terms of the level of acceptance or rejection. So, a simple two-step process seems inadequate to explain mass media influences, adequately.

Agenda Setting Theory

McCombs and Shaw advanced the agenda setting theory.

According to this theory the media makes an attempt to suggest ideas or indicate the relative importance of certain thoughts or issues. Upon receiving these messages, the audience then makes a selection in terms of their own preferences and priorities. The role of mass media communication is therefore seen as only setting an Agenda. How this agenda or theme is taken up and responded to is done by audience in keeping with their needs, interests, exposure, attitudes and so on.

Setting the agenda is like bringing into focus certain issues. Once this is done then the audience acts on the suggestions that have been made. To this extent media can be viewed as manipulating the audience. The audience is credited with being able to determine for themselves whether the agendas set by the media are acceptable or not. The level of acceptance or rejection determines the extent of influence the agenda set by the mass media has been able to create.

Social Cognitive Theory

Social cognitive theory provides an agentic conceptual framework within which to examine the determinants and mechanisms of such effects. Human behavior has often been explained in terms of unidirectional causation, in which behavior is shaped and controlled either by environmental influences or by internal dispositions.

Social cognitive theory explains psychosocial functioning in terms of triadic reciprocal causation. In this transactional view of self and society, personal factors in the form of cognitive, affective, and biological events; behavioral patterns; and environmental events all operate as interacting determinants that influence each other bidirectionally.

Social cognitive theory is founded in an agentic perspective.

People are self-organizing, proactive, self-reflecting, and self-regulating, not just reactive organisms shaped and shepherded by environmental events or inner forces. Human selfdevelopment, adaptation, and change are embedded in social systems. Therefore, personal agency operates within a broad network of sociostructural influences. In these agentic transactions, people are producers as well as products of social systems. Personal agency and social structure operate as codeterminants in an integrated causal structure rather than as a disembodied duality.

Seen from the sociocognitive perspective, human nature is a vast potentiality that can be fashioned by direct and observational experience into a variety of forms within biological limits. To say that a major distinguishing mark of humans is their endowed plasticity is not to say that they have no nature or that they come structureless . The plasticity, which is intrinsic to the nature of humans, depends upon neurophysiological mechanisms and structures that have evolved over time. These advanced neural systems specialized for processing, retaining, and using coded information provide the capacity for the very capabilities that are distinctly human- -generative symbolization, forethought, evaluative self- regulation, reflective self-consciousness, and symbolic communication.

Symbolic Capability

Social cognitive theory accords a central role to cognitive, vicarious, self-regulatory, and self-reflective processes. An extraordinary capacity for symbolization provides humans with a powerful tool for comprehending their environment and creating and regulating environmental events that touch virtually every aspect of their lives. Most external influences affect behavior through cognitive processes rather than directly.

Cognitive factors partly determine which environmental

events will be observed, what meaning will be conferred on them, whether they leave any lasting effects, what emotional impact and motivating power they will have, and how the information they convey will be organized for future use. It is with symbols that people process and transform transient experiences into cognitive models that serve as guides for judgment and action. Through symbols, people give meaning, form, and continuity to their experiences.

People gain understanding of causal relationships and expand their knowledge by operating symbolically on the wealth of information derived from personal and vicarious experiences. They generate solutions to problems, evaluate their likely outcomes, and pick suitable options without having to go through a laborious behavioral search.

Through the medium of symbols people can communicate with others at any distance in time and space. However, in keeping with the interactional perspective, social cognitive theory devotes much attention to the social origins of thought and the mechanisms through which social factors exert their influence on cognitive functioning. The other distinctive human capabilities are founded on this advanced capacity for symbolization.

Self-regulatory Capablity

People are not only knowers and performers. They are also self-reactors with a capacity for self-direction. Effective functioning requires the substitution of self-regulation for external sanctions and demands. The self-regulation of motivation, affect and action operates partly through internal standards and evaluative reactions to one's own behavior.

The anticipated self-satisfaction gained from fulfilling valued standards and discontent with substandard performances serve as incentive motivators for action. The motivational effects do not stem from the standards themselves, but from the evaluative self-investment in activities and positive and negative reactions to one's performances.

Most theories of self-regulation are founded on a negative feedback system in which people strive to reduce disparities between their perceived performance and an adopted standard. But self-regulation by negative discrepancy tells only half the story and not necessarily the more interesting half. In fact, people are proactive, aspiring organisms.

Human self-regulation relies on *discrepancy production* as well as *discrepancy reduction*. People motivate and guide their actions through proactive control by setting themselves challenging goals and then mobilizing their resources, skills and effort to fulfill them. After people attain the goal they have been pursuing, those with a strong sense of efficacy set higher goals for themselves. Adopting further challenges creates new motivating discrepancies to be mastered.

Self-regulation of motivation and action thus involves a dual control process of disequilibrating discrepancy production (proactive control) followed by equilibrating discrepancy reduction (reactive control). In areas of functioning involving achievement strivings and cultivation of competencies, the internal standards that are selected as a mark of adequacy are progressively altered as knowledge and skills are acquired and challenges are met. In many areas of social and moral behavior the internal standards that serve as the basis for regulating one's conduct have greater stability.

People do not change from week to week what they regard as right or wrong or good or bad. After they adopt a standard of morality, their self-sanctions for actions that match or violate their personal standards serve as the regulatory influencers. The exercise of moral agency has dual aspects—inhibitive and proactive. The *inhibitive* form is manifested in the power to refrain from behaving inhumanely. The *proactive* form of morality is expressed in the power to behave humanely.

The capability of forethought adds another dimension to the temporal extension of personal agency. Most human behavior is directed by forethought toward events and outcomes projected into the future. The future time perspective manifests itself in many different ways. People set goals for themselves, anticipate the likely consequences of their prospective actions, and otherwise plan courses of action that are likely to produce desired outcomes and to avoid undesired ones.

Because future events have no actual existence they cannot be causes of current motivation and action. However, by being represented cognitively in the present, conceived futures can operate anticipatorily as motivators and regulators of current behavior. When projected over a long time course on matters of value, a forethoughtful perspective provides direction, coherence, and meaning to one's life.

Self-reflective Capability

The capability to reflect upon oneself and the adequacy of one's thoughts and actions is another distinctly human attribute that figures prominently in social cognitive theory. People are not only agents of action but self-examiners of their functioning.

Effective cognitive functioning requires reliable ways of distinguishing between accurate and faulty thinking. In verifying thought by self-reflective means, people generate ideas, act on them or predict occurrences from them. They then judge from the results the adequacy of their thoughts, and change them accordingly. The validity and functional value of one's thoughts are evaluated by comparing how well thoughts match some indicant of reality.

Four different modes of thought verification can be distinguished. They include enactive, vicarious, social, and logical forms.

Enactive verification relies on the adequacy of the fit between one's thoughts and the results of the actions they spawn. Good matches corroborate thoughts; mismatches tend to refute them.

In *vicarious verification*, observing other people's transactions with the environment and the effects they produce provides a check on the correctness of one's own thinking. Vicarious thought verification is not simply a supplement to enactive experience. Symbolic modeling greatly expands the range of verification experiences that cannot otherwise be attained by personal action.

When experiential verification is difficult or unfeasible, *social verification* is used, with people evaluating the soundness of their views by checking them against what others believe.

In *logical verification* people can check for fallacies in their thinking by deducing from knowledge that is known what necessarily follows from it.

Such metacognitive activities usually foster veridical thought, but they can produce faulty thinking as well. Forceful actions arising from erroneous beliefs often create social environments that confirm the misbeliefs. We are all acquainted with problemprone individuals who, through offensive behavior, predictively breed negative social climates wherever they go.

Verification of thought by comparison with distorted media versions of social reality can foster shared misconceptions of people, places, and things. Social verification can foster bizarre views of reality if the shared beliefs of the reference group with which one affiliates are peculiar and the group is encapsulated from outside social ties and influences. Deductive reasoning can lead one astray if the propositional knowledge on which it is based is faulty or biases intrude on logical reasoning processes.

Among the self-referent thought none is more central or pervasive than people's belief in their efficacy to exert control over their level of functioning and events that affect their lives. This core belief is the foundation of human agency. Unless people believe that they can produce desired effects and forestall undesired ones by their actions, they have little incentive to act. Efficacy beliefs influence whether people think self-enhancingly or self-debilitatingly, optimistically or pessimistically; what courses of action they choose to pursue; the goals they set for themselves and their commitment to them; how much effort they put forth in given endeavors; the outcomes they expect their efforts to produce; how long they persevere in the face of obstacles; their resilience to adversity; how much stress and depression they experience in coping with taxing environmental demands; and the accomplishments they realize.

People do not live their lives in individual autonomy. They have to work together to secure what they cannot accomplish on their own. Social cognitive theory extends the conception of human agency to collective agency. The more efficacious groups judge themselves to be, the higher their collective aspirations, the greater their motivational investment in their undertakings, the stronger their staying power in the face of impediments, the more robust their resilience to adversity, and the higher their performance accomplishments.

Vicarious Capability

Psychological theories have traditionally emphasized learning by the effects of one's actions. If knowledge and skills could be acquired only by response consequences human development would be greatly retarded, not to mention exceedingly tedious and hazardous. A culture could never transmit its language, mores, social practices, and requisite competencies if they had to be shaped tediously in each new member by response consequences without the benefit of models to exemplify the cultural patterns. Shortening the acquisition process is vital for survival as well as for self-development because natural endowment provides few inborn skills, hazards are ever present, and errors can be perilous. Moreover, the constraints of time, resources, and mobility impose severe limits on the places and activities that can be directly explored for the acquisition of new knowledge and competencies.

Humans have evolved an advanced capacity for observational learning that enables them to expand their knowledge and skills rapidly through information conveyed by the rich variety of models. Indeed, virtually all behavioral, cognitive, and affective learning from direct experience can be achieved vicariously by observing people's actions and its consequences for them. Much social learning occurs either designedly or unintentionally from models in one's immediate environment. However, a vast amount of information about human values, styles of thinking, and behavior patterns is gained from the extensive modeling in the symbolic environment of the mass media.

A major significance of symbolic modeling lies in its tremendous reach and psychosocial impact. Unlike learning by doing, which requires altering the actions of each individual through repeated trial-and-error experiences, in observational learning a single model can transmit new ways of thinking and behaving simultaneously to countless people in widely dispersed locales.

There is another aspect of symbolic modeling that magnifies its psychological and social impact. During the course of their daily lives, people have direct contact with only a small sector of the physical and social environment. They work in the same setting, travel the same routes, visit the same places, and see the same set of friends and associates. Consequently, their conceptions of social reality are greatly influenced by vicarious experiences—by what they see, hear, and read— without direct experiential correctives. To a large extent, people act on their images of reality. The more people's images of reality depend upon the media's symbolic environment, the greater is its social impact.

Most psychological theories were cast long before the advent of extraordinary advances in the technology of communication. As a result, they give insufficient attention to the increasingly powerful role that the symbolic environment plays in present-day human lives. Whereas previously, modeling influences were largely confined to the behavior patterns exhibited in one's immediate environment, the accelerated growth of video delivery technologies has vastly expanded the range of models to which members of society are exposed day in and day out.

By drawing on these modeled patterns of thought and behavior, observers can transcend the bounds of their immediate environment. New ideas, values, behavior patterns and social practices are now being rapidly diffused by symbolic modeling worldwide in ways that foster a globally distributed consciousness. Because the symbolic environment occupies a major part of people's everyday lives, much of the social construction of reality and shaping of public consciousness occurs through electronic acculturation. At the societal level, the electronic modes of influence are transforming how social systems operate and serving as a major vehicle for sociopolitical change.

Observational Learning

Attentional processes determine what is selectively observed in the profusion of modeling influences and what information is extracted from ongoing modeled events. A number of factors influence the exploration and construal of what is modeled. Some of these determinants concern the cognitive skills, preconceptions and value preferences of the observers.

Others are related to the salience, attractiveness, and functional value of the modeled activities themselves. Still other factors are the structural arrangements of human interactions and associational networks, which largely determine the types of models to which people have ready access.

People cannot be much influenced by observed events if they do not remember them. A second major subfunction governing observational learning concerns cognitive representational processes. Retention involves an active process of transforming and restructuring information conveyed by modeled events into rules and conceptions for memory representation. Retention is greatly aided by symbolic transformations of modeled information into memory codes and cognitive rehearsal of the coded information.

Preconceptions and affective states exert biasing influences on these representational activities. Similarly, recall involves a process of reconstruction rather than simply retrieval of registered events. In the third subfunction in modeling—the behavioral production process—symbolic conceptions are translated into appropriate courses of action. This is achieved through a conception-matching process in which conceptions guide the construction and execution of behavior patterns which are then compared against the conceptual model for adequateness. The behavior is modified on the basis of the comparative information to achieve close correspondence between conception and action.

The mechanism for translating cognition into action involves both transformational and generative operations. Execution of a skill must be constantly varied to suit changing circumstances. Adaptive performance, therefore, requires a generative conception rather than a one-to-one mapping between cognitive representation and action. By applying an abstract specification of the activity, people can produce many variations on the skill. Conceptions are rarely transformed into masterful performance on the first attempt.

Monitored enactments serve as the vehicle for transforming knowledge into skilled action. Performances are perfected by corrective adjustments during behavior production. The more extensive the subskills that people possess, the easier it is to integrate them to produce new behavior patterns. When deficits exist, the subskills required for complex performances must first be developed by modeling and guided enactment.

The fourth subfunction in modeling concerns motivational processes. Social cognitive theory distinguishes between acquisition and performance because people do not perform everything they learn. Performance of observationally learned behavior is influenced by three major types of incentive motivators—direct, vicarious, and self-produced. People are more likely to exhibit modeled behavior if it results in valued outcomes than if it has unrewarding or punishing effects.

The observed detriments and benefits experienced by others influence the performance of modeled patterns in much the same way as do directly experienced consequences. People are motivated by the successes of others who are similar to themselves, but are discouraged from pursuing courses of behavior that they have seen often result in adverse consequences. Personal standards of conduct provide a further source of incentive motivation.

The self-approving and self-censuring reactions people generate to their own behavior regulate which observationally learned activities they are most likely to pursue. They pursue activities they find self-satisfying and give them a sense of worth but reject those they personally disapprove.

The different sources of consequences may operate as complimentary or opposing influences on behavior. Behavior patterns are most firmly established when social and self-sanctions are compatible. Under such conditions, socially approvable behavior is a source of self-pride and socially disapprovable behavior is self-censured. Behavior is especially susceptible to external influences in the absence of countervailing self-sanctions.

People who are not much committed to personal standards adopt a pragmatic orientation, tailoring their behavior to fit whatever the situation seems to call for. They become adept at reading social situations and guiding their actions by expediency. One type of conflict between social and self-produced sanctions arises when individuals are socially punished for behavior they highly value.

Principled dissenters and nonconformists often find themselves in this predicament. Here, the relative strength of self-approval and social censure determine whether the behavior will be restrained or expressed. Should the threatened social consequences be severe, people hold in check self-praiseworthy acts in risky situations but perform them readily in relatively safe settings. These are individuals, however, whose sense of self-worth is so strongly invested in certain convictions that they will submit to prolonged maltreatment rather than accede to what they regard as unjust or immoral.

People commonly experience conflicts in which they are socially pressured to engage in behavior that violates their moral standards. When self-devaluative consequences outweigh the benefits for socially accommodating behavior, the social influences do not have much sway. However, the self-regulation of conduct operates through conditional application of moral standards. We shall see shortly that self-sanctions can be weakened or nullified by selective disengagement of internal control.

Abstract Modeling

Modeling is not merely a process of behavioral mimicry, a commonly misconstrued. The proven skills and established customs of a culture may be adopted in essentially the same form as they are exemplified because of their high functional value. However, in most activities, subskills must be improvised to suit varying circumstances.

Modeling influences convey rules for generative and innovative behavior as well. This higher-level learning is achieved through abstract modeling. Rule-governed judgments and actions differ in specific content and other details while embodying the same underlying rule. For example, a model may confront moral conflicts that differ widely in content but apply the same moral standard to them. In this higher form of abstract modeling, observers extract the rule governing the specific judgments or actions exhibited by others. Once they learn the rule, they can use it to judge or generate new instances of behavior that go beyond what they have seen or heard.

Much human learning is aimed at developing cognitive skills on how to gain and use knowledge for future use. Observational learning of thinking skills is greatly facilitated by having models verbalize their thoughts aloud as they engage in problem-solving activities. The thoughts guiding their decisions and action strategies are thus made observable for adoption.

Acquiring generative rules from modeled information involves at least three processes:extracting the generic features from various social exemplars; integrating the extracted information into composite rules; and using the rules to produce new instances of behavior. Through abstract modeling, people acquire, among other things, standards for categorizing and judging events, linguistic rules of communication, thinking skills on how to gain and use knowledge, and personal standards for regulating one's motivation and conduct.

Evidence that generative rules of thought and conduct can be created through abstract modeling attests to the broad scope of observational learning. Modeling also plays a prominent role in creativity. Creativeness rarely springs entirely from individual inventiveness. By refining preexisting innovations, synthesizing them into new procedures and adding novel elements, something new is created. When exposed to models of differing styles of thinking and behaving, observers vary in what they adopt and thereby create new blends of personal characteristics that differ from the individual models. Modeling new perspectives and innovative styles of thinking also fosters creativity by weakening conventional mind sets.

Motivational Effects

Social cognitive theory distinguishes among several modeling functions, each governed by different determinants and underlying mechanisms. In addition to cultivating new competencies, modeling influences have strong motivational effects. Vicarious motivators are rooted in outcome expectations formed from information conveyed by the rewarding and punishing outcomes of modeled courses of action. Seeing others gain desired outcomes by their actions can create outcome expectancies that function as positive incentives; observed punishing outcomes can create negative outcome expectancies that function as disincentives. These motivational effects are governed by observers' judgments of their ability to accomplish the modeled behavior, their perception of the modeled actions as producing favorable or adverse consequences, and their inferences that similar or unlike consequences would result if they, themselves, were to engage in similar activities.

Vicarious incentives take on added significance by their power to alter the valence and force of external incentives. The value of a given outcome is largely determined by its relation to other outcomes rather than inheres in their intrinsic qualities. The same outcome can function as a reward or punisher depending on social comparison between observed and personally experienced outcomes. For example, the same pay raise has negative valence for persons who have seen similar performances by others compensated more generously, but positive valence when others have been compensated less generously.

Equitable rewards foster a sense of well-being; inequitable one's breed discontent and resentment. Vicariously created motivators have been studied most extensively in terms of the inhibitory and disinhibitory effects of modeled transgressive, aggressive and sexual behavior with accompanying outcomes.

Transgressive behavior is regulated by two major sources of sanctions—social sanctions and internalized self-sanctions. Both control mechanisms operate anticipatorily. In motivators arising from social sanctions, people refrain from transgressing because they anticipate that such conduct will bring them social censure and other adverse consequences. In motivators rooted in self-reactive control, people refrain from transgressing because such conduct will give rise to self-reproach.

Media portrayals can alter perceived social sanctions by the way in which the consequences of different styles of conduct are portrayed. For example, televised aggression is often exemplified in ways that tend to weaken restraints over aggressive conduct. In televised representations of human discord, physical aggression is a preferred solution to interpersonal conflicts; it is acceptable and relatively successful; and it is socially sanctioned by superheroes triumphing over evil by violent means. Such portrayals legitimize, glamorize and trivialize human violence.

Inhibitory and disinhibitory effects stemming from self-sanctions are mediated largely through self-regulatory mechanisms. After standards have been internalized, they serve as guides and deterrents to conduct by the self-approving and self-reprimanding consequences people produce for themselves. However, moral standards do not function as fixed internal regulators of conduct. Self-regulatory mechanisms do not operate unless they are activated, and there are many processes by which moral reactions can be disengaged from inhumane conduct. Selective activation and disengagement of internal control permits different types of conduct with the same moral standards.

One set of disengagement practices operates on the construal of the behavior itself by *moral justification*. People do not ordinarily engage in reprehensible conduct until they have justified to themselves the morality of their actions. What is culpable is made personally and socially acceptable by portraying it in the service of moral purposes. Moral justification is widely used to support self-serving and otherwise culpable conduct. Moral judgments of conduct are also partly influenced by what it is compared against. Self-deplored acts can be made benign or honorable by contrasting them with more flagrant transgressions.

Since examples of human culpability abound, they lend themselves readily to cognitive restructuring of transgressive conduct by such *advantageous comparison*. Activities can take on a very different appearance depending on what they are called. Sanitizing *euphemistic labeling* provides another convenient device for masking reprehensible activities or even conferring a respectable status upon them. Through convoluted verbiage, reprehensible conduct is made benign and those who engage in it are relieved of a sense of personal agency.

Cognitive restructuring of behavior through moral justifications and palliative characterizations is the most effective psychological mechanism for promoting transgressive conduct. This is because moral restructuring not only eliminates self-deterrents but engages selfapproval in the service of transgressive exploits. What was once morally condemnable becomes a source of self-valuation.

Ball-Rokeach attaches special significance to evaluative reactions and social justifications presented in the media, particularly in conflicts of power. This is because relatively few viewers experience sufficient inducement to use the aggressive strategies they have seen, but the transmitted justifications and evaluations can help to mobilize public support for policy actions favoring either social control or social change. The justificatory changes can have widespread social and political ramifications.

The mass media, especially television, provide the best access to the public through its strong drawing power. For this reason, television is increasingly used as the principle vehicle of justification. Struggles to legitimize and gain support for one's values and causes and to discredit those of one's opponents are now waged more and more through the electronic media.

Because of its potential influence, the communication system itself is subject to constant pressures from different factions within society seeking to sway it to their ideology. Research on the role of the mass media in the social construction of reality carries important social implications.

Self-sanctions are activated most strongly when personal

causation of detrimental effects is apparent. Another set of disengagement practices operates by obscuring or distorting the relationship between actions and the effects they cause. People will behave in ways they normally repudiate if a legitimate authority sanctions their conduct and accepts responsibility for its consequences.

Under conditions of *displacement of responsibility*, people view their actions as springing from the dictates of others rather than their being personally responsible for them. Since they are not the actual agent of their actions, they are spared selfprohibiting reactions. The deterrent power of self-sanctions is also weakened when the link between conduct and its consequences is obscured by *diffusion of responsibility* for culpable behavior. Through division of labor, diffusion of decision making, and group action, people can behave detrimentally without any one person feeling personally responsible. People behave more injuriously under diffused responsibility than when they hold themselves personally accountable for what they do.

Additional ways of weakening self-deterring reactions operate through *disregard or distortion of the consequences of action*. When people pursue detrimental activities for personal gain or because of social inducements, they avoid facing the harm they cause or they minimize it. They readily recall the possible benefits of the behavior but are less able to remember its harmful effects. In addition to selective inattention and cognitive distortion of effects, the misrepresentation may involve active efforts to discredit evidence of the harm they cause.

As long as the detrimental results of one's conduct are ignored, minimized, distorted, or disbelieved there is little reason for self-censure to be activated. The final set of disengagement practices operates at the point of recipients of detrimental acts.

The strength of self- evaluative reactions to detrimental conduct partly depends on how the perpetrators view the people toward whom the behavior is directed.

To perceive another as human enhances empathetic or vicarious reactions through perceived similarity. As a result, it is difficult to mistreat humanized persons without risking self-condemnation. Selfsanctions against cruel conduct can be disengaged or blunted by *dehumanization*, which divests people of human qualities or invests them with bestial qualities. While dehumanization weakens self-restraints against cruel conduct, humanization fosters considerate, compassionate behavior.

Attribution of blame to one's antagonists is still another expedient that can serve selfexonerative purposes. Deleterious interactions usually involve a series of reciprocally escalative actions, in which the antagonists are rarely faultless. One can always select from the chain of events an instance of the adversary's defensive behavior and view it as the original instigation. Injurious conduct thus becomes a justifiable defensive reaction to belligerent provocations. Others can, therefore, be blamed for bringing suffering on themselves. Self-exoneration is similarly achievable by viewing one's detrimental conduct as forced by circumstances rather than as a personal decision.

By blaming others or circumstances, not only are one's own actions excusable but one can even feel self- righteous in the process. Because internalized controls can be selectively activated and disengaged, marked changes in moral conduct can be achieved without changing people's personality structures, moral principles, or self-evaluative systems. It is self-exonerative processes rather than character flaws that account for most inhumanities. The massive threats to human welfare stem mainly from deliberate acts of principle rather than from unrestrained acts of impulse. Research in which the different disengagement factors are systematically varied in media portrayals of inhumanities attests to the disinhibitory power of mass media influences.

Viewers' punitiveness is enhanced by exposure to media productions that morally justify injurious conduct, blame and dehumanize victims, displace or diffuse personal responsibility, and sanitize destructive consequences. Research assessing self-reactive control provides evidence that sanctioning social conditions are linked to self-regulatory influences which, in turn, are linked to injurious conduct. The same disengagement mechanisms are enlisted heavily by members of the television industry in the production of programs that exploit human brutality for commercial purposes.

Acquisition and Modification of Affective Dispositions

People are easily aroused by the emotional expressions of others. Vicarious arousal operates mainly through an intervening self-arousal process. That is, seeing others react emotionally to instigating conditions activates emotion-arousing thoughts and imagery in observers. As people develop their capacity for cognitive self-arousal, they can generate emotional reactions to cues that are only suggestive of a model's emotional experiences. Conversely, they can neutralize or attenuate the emotional impact of modeled distress by thoughts that transform threatening situations into nonthreatening ones.

If the affective reactions of models only aroused observers fleetingly, it would be of some interest as far as momentary communication is concerned, but of limited psychological import. What gives significance to vicarious influence is that observers can acquire lasting attitudes, emotional reactions, and behavioral proclivities toward persons, places, or things that have been associated with modeled emotional experiences. They learn to fear the things that frightened models, to dislike what repulsed them, and to like what gratified them.

Fears and intractable phobias are ameliorated by modeling influences that convey information about coping strategies for exercising control over the things that are feared. The stronger the instilled sense of coping self-efficacy, the bolder the behavior. Values can similarly be developed and altered vicariously by repeated exposure to modeled preferences.

Social Construction of Reality

Televised representations of social realities reflect ideological bents in their portrayal of human nature, social relations, and the norms and structure of society. Heavy exposure to this symbolic world may eventually make the televised images appear to be the authentic state of human affairs. Some disputes about the vicarious cultivation of beliefs has arisen over findings from correlational studies using global indices based on amount of television viewing.

Televised influence is best defined in terms of the contents people watch rather than the sheer amount of television viewing. More particularized measures of exposure to the televised fare show that heavy television viewing shapes viewers' beliefs and conceptions of reality. The relationship remains when other possible contributing factors are simultaneously controlled.

Vicarious cultivation of social conceptions is most clearly revealed in studies verifying the direction of causality by varying experimentally the nature and amount of exposure to media influences. Controlled laboratory studies provide converging evidence that television portrayals shape viewer's beliefs. Portrayals in the print media similarly shape conceptions of social reality.

To see the world as the televised messages portray it is to

harbor some misconceptions. Indeed, many of the shared misconceptions about occupational pursuits, ethnic groups, minorities, the elderly, social and sex roles, and other aspects of life are at least partly cultivated through symbolic modeling of stereotypes. Verification of personal conceptions against televised versions of social reality can thus foster some collective illusions.

Social Promoting of Human Behaviour

The actions of others can also serve as social prompts for previously learned behavior that observers can perform but have not done so because of insufficient inducements, rather than because of restraints. Social prompting effects are distinguished from observational learning and disinhibition because no new behavior has been acquired, and disinhibitory processes are not involved because the elicited behavior is socially acceptable and not encumbered by restraints.

The influence of models in activating, channeling, and supporting the behavior of others is abundantly documented in both laboratory and field studies. By exemplification one can get people to behave altruistically, to volunteer their services, to delay or seek gratification, to show affection, to select certain foods and drinks, to choose certain kinds of apparel, to converse on particular topics, to be inquisitive or passive, to think creatively or conventionally, or to engage in other permissible courses of action.

Thus, the types of models who predominate within a social milieu partly determine which human qualities, from among many alternatives, are selectively activated. The actions of models acquire the power to activate and channel behavior when they are good predictors for observers that positive results can be gained by similar conduct.

The fashion and taste industries rely heavily on the social

prompting power of modeling. Because the potency of vicarious influences can be enhanced by showing modeled acts bringing rewards, vicarious outcomes figure prominently in advertising campaigns. Thus, drinking a certain brand of wine or using a particular shampoo wins the loving admiration of beautiful people, enhances job performance, masculinizes self-conception, actualizes individualism and authenticity, tranquilizes irritable nerves, invites social recognition and amicable reactions from total strangers, and arouses affectionate overtures from spouses.

The types of vicarious outcomes, model characteristics, and modeling formats that are selected vary depending on what happens to be in vogue at the time. Model characteristics are varied to boost the persuasiveness of commercial messages. Prestigeful models are often enlisted to capitalize on the high regard in which they are held. The best social sellers depend on what happens to be popular at the moment.

Drawing on evidence that similarity to the model enhances modeling, some advertisements portray common folk achieving wonders with the wares advertised. Because vicarious influence increases with multiplicity of modeling, the beers, soft drinks, and snacks are being consumed with gusto in the advertised world by groups of wholesome, handsome, fun-loving models. Eroticism is another stimulant that never goes out of style. Therefore, erotic modeling does heavy duty in efforts to command attention and to make advertised products more attractive to potential buyers.

In sum, modeling influences serve diverse functions—as tutors, motivators, inhibitors, disinhibitors, social prompters, emotion arousers, and shapers of values and conceptions of reality. Although the different modeling functions can operate separately, in nature they often work in concert. Thus, for example, in the spread of new styles of aggression, models serve as both teachers and disinhibitors. When novel conduct is punished, observers learn the conduct that was punished as well as the restraints.

Multi-pattern Flow of Influence

It has been commonly assumed in theories of mass communication that modeling influences operate through a two-step diffusion process. Influential persons pick up new ideas from the media and pass them on to their followers through personal influence. Some communication researchers have claimed that the media can only reinforce preexisting styles of behavior but cannot create new ones. Such a view is at variance with a vast body of evidence. Media influences create personal attributes as well as alter preexisting ones.

The different modes of human influence are too diverse in nature to have a fixed path of influence or strengths. Most behavior is the product of multiple determinants operating in concert. Hence, the relative contribution of any given factor in a pattern of influences can change depending on the nature and strength of coexisting determinants. Even the same determinant operating within the same causal structure of factors can change in its causal contribution with further experience.

In the case of atypical behavior, it is usually produced by a unique constellation of the determinants, such that if any one of them were absent the behavior would not have occurred. Depending on their quality and coexistence of other determinants, media influences may be subordinate to, equal to, or outweigh nonmedia influences. Given the dynamic nature of multifaceted causal structures, efforts to affix an average strength to a given mode of influence calls to mind the nonswimming analyst who drowned while trying to cross a river that averaged three feet in depth.

The view that the path of media influence is exclusively a filter-down process is disputed by a wealth of knowledge regarding modeling influences. Human judgment, values and conduct can be altered directly by televised modeling without having to wait for an influential intermediary to adopt what has been shown and then to serve as the diffuser to others.

Watt and van den Berg tested several alternative theories about how media communications relate to public attitudes and behavior. The explanatory contenders included the conceptions that media influence people directly; media influence opinion leaders who then affect others; media have no independent effects; media set the public agenda for discussions by designating what is important but do not otherwise influence the public; and finally, media simply reflect public attitudes and behavior rather than shape them.

The direct-flow model from media to the public received the best empirical support. In this study, the behavior was highly publicized and could bring benefits without risks. When the activities being advocated require the investment of time and resources, and failures can be costly, people are inclined to seek verification of functional value from other sources as well before they act.

Chaffee reviews substantial evidence that calls into question the prevailing view that interpersonal sources of information are necessarily more persuasive than media sources. People seek information that may be potentially useful to them from different sources. Neither informativeness, credibility, nor persuasiveness are uniquely tied to interpersonal sources or to media sources. How extensively different sources are used depends, in large part, on their accessibility and the likelihood that they will provide the kinds of information sought.

Modeling affects the adoption of new social practices and behavior patterns in several ways. It instructs people about new ways of thinking and behaving by informative demonstration or description. Learning about new things does not rely on a fixed hierarchy of sources. Efficacious modeling not only cultivates competencies but also enhances the sense of personal efficacy needed to transform knowledge and skills into successful courses of action.

The relative importance of interpersonal and media sources of information in initiating the adoption process varies for different activities and for the same activity at different stages in the adoption process. Models motivate as well as inform and enable. People are initially reluctant to adopt new practices that involve costs and risks until they see the advantages that have been gained by early adopters. Modeled benefits accelerate social diffusion by weakening the restraints of the more cautious potential adopters.

As acceptance spreads, the new ways gain further social support. Models also display preferences and evaluative reactions, which can alter observers' values and standards. Changes in evaluative standards affect receptivity to the activities being modeled. Models not only exemplify and legitimate new practices, they also serve as advocates for them by directly encouraging others to adopt them. In effecting large-scale changes, communications systems operate through two pathways.

In the direct pathway, communications media promote changes by informing, modeling, motivating, and guiding participants. In the socially-mediated pathway, media influences are used to link participants to social networks and community settings. These places provide continued personalized guidance, as well as natural incentives and social supports for desired changes. The major share of behavior changes is promoted within these social milieus.

The absence of individualized guidance limits the power of one-way mass communications. The revolutionary advances in interactive technologies provide the means to expand the reach and impact of communications media. On the input side, communications can now be personally tailored to factors that are causally related to the behavior of interest.

Tailored communications are viewed as more relevant and credible, are better remembered and are more effective in influencing behavior than general messages. On the behavioral guidance side, interactive technologies provide a convenient means of individualizing the type and level of behavioral guidance needed to bring desired changes to fruition.

In the population-based approaches the communications are designed to inform, enable, motivate, and guide people to effect personal and social changes. In implementing the social linking function, communications media can connect people to interactive online self-management programs that provide intensive individualized guidance in their homes when they want it. In short, there is no single pattern of social influence.

The media can implant ideas either directly or through adopters. Analyses of the role of mass media in social diffusion must distinguish between their effect on learning modeled activities and on their adoptive use, and examine how media and interpersonal influences affect these separable processes. In some instances the media both teach new forms of behavior and create motivators for action by altering people's value preferences, efficacy beliefs, outcome expectations, and perception of opportunity structures.

In other instances, the media teach but other adopters provide the incentive motivation to perform what has been learned observationally. In still other instances, the effect of the media may be entirely socially mediated. That is, people who have had no exposure to the media are influenced by adopters who have had the exposure and then, themselves, become the transmitters of the new ways. Within these different patterns of social influence, the media can serve as originating, as well as reinforcing, influences. The hierarchical pattern is more likely to obtain for the print media, which has a more limited audience, than for the ubiquitous video media.

Communication technologies and global interconnectedness provide people with ready direct access to information worldwide independently of time and place and unfettered by institutional and moneyed gatekeepers. The public is less dependent on a mediated filter-down system of persuasion and enlightenment. These vastly expanded opportunities for self-directedness underscore the growing primacy of agentic initiative in human adaptation and change in the electronic era.

Ready access to communication technologies will not necessarily enlist active participation unless people believe that they can achieve desired results by this means. Perceived personal and collective efficacy partly determines the extent to which people use this resource and the purposes to which they put it.

Social Diffusion through Symbolic Modelling

Much of the preceding discussion has been concerned mainly with modeling at the individual level. A unique property of modeling is that it can transmit information of virtually limitless variety to vast numbers of people simultaneously through the medium of symbolic modeling. Extraordinary advances in technology of communication are transforming the nature, reach, speed and loci of human influenc.

These technological developments have radically altered the social diffusion process. The video system feeding off telecommunications satellites has become the dominant vehicle for disseminating symbolic environments. Social practices are not only being widely diffused within societies, but ideas, values, and styles of conduct are being modeled worldwide. The electronic media are coming to play an increasingly influential role in transcultural change. Televised modeling is now being used to effect social change at community and society-wide levels.

Social cognitive theory analyzes social diffusion of new behavior patterns in terms of three constituent processes and the psychosocial factors that govern them. These include the acquisition of knowledge about innovative behaviors; the adoption of these behaviors in practice; and the social networks through which they spread and are supported. Diffusion of innovation follows a common pattern.

New ideas and social practices are introduced by notable example. Initially, the rate of adoption is slow because new ways are unfamiliar, customs resist change and results are uncertain. As early adopters convey more information about how to apply the new practices and their potential benefits, the innovation is adopted at an accelerating rate. After a period in which the new practices spread rapidly, the rate of diffusion slows down. The use of the innovation then either stabilizes or declines, depending upon its relative functional value.

Symbolic modeling usually functions as the principal conveyer of innovations to widely dispersed areas. This is especially true in the early stages of diffusion. Newspapers, magazines, radio, and television inform people about new practices and their likely risks or benefits. The Internet provides instant communicative access worldwide. Early adopters, therefore, come from among those who have had greater access to media sources of information about innovations.

The psychosocial determinants and mechanisms of observational learning, which were reviewed earlier, govern the rate with which innovations are acquired. Differences in the knowledge, skills and resources particular innovations require produce variations in rate of acquisition. Innovations that are difficult to understand and use receive more reluctant consideration than simpler ones.

When television models new practices on the screens in virtually every household, people in widely dispersed locales can learn them. However, not all innovations are promoted through the mass media. Some rely on informal personal channels. In such instances, physical proximity determines which innovations will be repeatedly observed and thoroughly learned.

It is one thing to acquire skills, it is another thing to use them effectively under difficult circumstances. Human competency requires not only skills, but also self-belief in one's capabilities to use those skills well. Modeling influences must, therefore, be designed to build self-efficacy as well as convey knowledge and rules of behavior. Perceived self-efficacy affects every phase of personal change. It determines whether people even consider changing their behavior, whether they can enlist the motivation and perseverance needed to succeed should they choose to do so, and how well they maintain the changes they have achieved.

The influential role of people's beliefs in their personal efficacy in social diffusion is shown in their response to health communications aimed at altering health-impairing habits. Meyerowitz and Chaiken examined four alternative mechanisms through which health communications could alter health habits by transmission of factual information, fear arousal, change in risk perception, and enhancement of perceived self- efficacy. They found that health communications fostered adoption of preventive health practices primarily by their effects on perceived self-efficacy.

Beck and Lund have similarly shown that preventive health practices are better promoted by heightening self-efficacy than by elevating fear. Analyses of how community-wide media campaigns produce changes reveal that both the preexisting and induced level of perceived self-efficacy play an influential role in the adoption and social diffusion of health practices.

The stronger the preexisting perceived self- efficacy, and the more the media campaigns enhance people's beliefs in their self-regulative efficacy, the more likely they are to adopt the recommended practices. Health knowledge gets translated into healthful habits through the mediation of perceived selfefficacy.

The acquisition of knowledge and skills regarding innovations is necessary, but not sufficient for their adoption in practice. A number of factors determine whether people will act on what they have learned. Environmental inducements serve as one set of regulators. Adoptive behavior is also highly susceptible to incentive influences, which may take the form of material, social, or self-evaluative outcomes. Some of the motivating incentives derive from the utility of the adoptive behavior. The greater the relative benefits provided by an innovation, the higher is the incentive to adopt it. However, benefits cannot be experienced until the new practices are tried. Promoters, therefore, strive to get people to adopt new practices by altering their preferences and beliefs about likely outcomes, mainly by enlisting vicarious incentives.

Advocates of new technologies and ideologies create expectations that they offer better solutions than established ways do. Modeled benefits increase adoptive decisions. Modeling influences can, of course, impede as well as promote the diffusion process. Modeling negative reactions to a particular innovation, as a result of having had disappointing experiences with it, dissuades others from trying it. Even modeled indifference to an innovation, in the absence of any personal experience with it, will dampen the interests of others.

Many innovations serve as a means of gaining social

recognition and status. Indeed, status incentives are often the main motivators for adopting new styles and tastes. In many instances, the variant styles do not provide different natural benefits or, if anything, the most innovative styles are the most costly. Status is thus gained at a price.

People who strive to distinguish themselves from the common and the ordinary adopt new styles in clothing, grooming, recreational activities, and conduct, thereby achieving distinctive social standing. As the popularity of the new behavior grows, it loses its status-conferring value until eventually it, too, becomes commonplace. It is then discarded for a new form.

Adoptive behavior is also partly governed by self-evaluative reactions to one's own behavior. People adopt what they value, but resist innovations that violate their social and moral standards or that conflict with their self-conception. The more compatible an innovation is with prevailing social norms and value systems, the greater its adoptability. However, we saw earlier that self-evaluative sanctions do not operate in isolation from the pressures of social influence. People are often led to behave in otherwise personally devalued ways by strategies that circumvent negative self-reactions. This is done by changing appearances and meanings of new practices to make them look compatible with people's values.

The amenability of an innovation to brief trial is another relevant characteristic that can affect the ease of adoption. Innovations that can be tried on a limited basis are more readily adoptable than those that have to be tried on a large scale with substantial effort and costs. The more weight given to potential risks and the costs of getting rid of new practices should they fail to live up to expectations, the weaker is the incentive to innovate. And finally, people will not adopt innovations even though they are favorably disposed toward them if they lack the money, the skills, or the accessory resources that may be needed.

The more resources innovations require, the lower is their adoptability.

Analysis of the determinants and mechanisms of social diffusion should not becloud the fact that not all innovations are useful, nor is resistance to them necessarily dysfunctional. In the continuous flow of innovations, the number of disadvantageous ones far exceeds those with truly beneficial possibilities. Both personal and societal well-being are well served by initial wariness to new practices promoted by unsubstantiated or exaggerated claims. The designations "venturesome" for early adopters and "laggards" for later adopters are fitting in the case of innovations that hold promise.

However, when people are mesmerized by alluring appeals into trying innovations of questionable value, the more suitable designation is gullibility for early adopters and astuteness for resisters. Rogers has criticized the prevalent tendency to conceptualize the diffusion process from the perspective of the promoters. This tends to bias the search for explanations of nonadoptive behavior in negative attributes of nonadopters.

§§§§The third major factor that affects the diffusion process concerns social network structures. People are enmeshed in networks of relationships that include occupational colleagues, organizational members, kinships, and friendships, just to mention a few. They are linked not only directly by personal relationships. Because acquaintanceships overlap different network clusters, many people become linked to each other indirectly by interconnected ties.

Social structures comprise clustered networks of people with various ties among them, as well as persons who provide connections to other clusters through joint membership or a liaison role. Clusters vary in their internal structure, ranging from loosely knit ones to those that are densely interconnected. Networks also differ in the number and pattern of structural linkages between clusters. They may have many common ties or function with a high degree of separateness. In addition to their degree of interconnectedness, people vary in the positions and status they occupy in particular social networks which can affect their impact on what spreads through their network. One is more apt to learn about new ideas and practices from brief contacts with causal acquaintances than from intensive contact in the same circle of close associates. This path of influence creates the seemingly paradoxical effect that innovations are extensively diffused to cohesive groups through weak social ties.

Information regarding new ideas and practices is often conveyed through multilinked relationships. Traditionally, the communication process has been conceptualized as one of unidirectional persuasion flowing from a source to a recipient. Rogers emphasizes the mutuality of influence in interpersonal communication. People share information, give meaning by mutual feedback to the information they exchange, gain understanding of each other's views, and influence each other. Specifying the channels of influence through which innovations are dispersed provides greater understanding of the diffusion process than simply plotting the rate of adoptions over time.

There is no single social network in a community that serves all purposes. Different innovations engage different networks. For example, birth control practices and agricultural innovations diffuse through quite different networks within the same community. To complicate matters further, the social networks that come into play in initial phases of diffusion may differ from those that spread the innovation in subsequent phases.

Adoption rates are better predicted from the network that subserves a particular innovation than from a more general communication network. This is not to say that there is no generality to the diffusion function of network structures. If a particular social structure subserves varied activities, it can help to spread the adoption of innovations in each of those activities.

People with many social ties are more apt to adopt innovations than those who have few ties to others. Adoption rates increase as more and more people in one's personal network adopt an innovation. The effects of social connectedness on adoptive behavior may be mediated through several processes.

Multilinked relations can foster adoption of innovations because they convey more factual information, they mobilize stronger social influences, or it may be that people with close ties are more receptive to new ideas than those who are socially estranged. Moreover, in social transactions, people see their associates adopt innovations as well as talk about them. Multiple modeling alone can increase adoptive behavior.

If innovations are highly conspicuous, they can be adopted directly without requiring interaction among adopters. Television is being increasingly used to forge large single-link structures, in which many people are linked directly to the media source, but they may have little or no direct relations with each other. For example, television evangelists attract loyal followers who adopt the transmitted precepts as guides for how to behave in situations involving moral, social and political issues.

Although they share a common bond to the media source, most members of an electronic community may never see each other. Political power structures are similarly being transformed by the creation of new constituencies tied to a single media source, but with little interconnectedness. Mass marketing techniques, using computer identification and mass mailings, create special-interest constituencies that by-pass traditional political organizations in the exercise of political influence.

The evolving information technologies will increasingly serve as a vehicle for building social networks. Online transactions transcend the barriers of time and space. Through interactive electronic networking people link together in widely dispersed locals, exchange information, share new ideas, and transact any number of pursuits. Virtual networking provides a flexible means for creating diffusion structures to serve given purposes, expanding their membership, extending them geographically, and disbanding them when they have outlived their usefulness.

Although structural interconnectedness provides potential diffusion paths, psychosocial factors largely determine the fate of what diffuses through those paths. In other words, it is the transactions that occur within social relationships rather than the ties, themselves, that explain adoptive behavior. The course of diffusion is best understood by considering the interactions among psychosocial determinants of adoptive behavior, the properties of innovations that facilitate or impede adoption, and the network structures that provide the social pathways of influence.

2

Communication Revolution

New media technologies promise profound changes in how global citizens obtain news and feature programming, as well as how we communicate among ourselves and contribute to the emerging decentralized, many-to-many media system. By becoming aware of how mass media is controlled and biased by a few corporations; by choosing alternative media sources; and by taking action to publish news and original content with digital production tools, the Internet and independent media vehicles - the public can create a true revolution in the control and presentation of media.

'Convergence' is the label most often used for the integration of communication mediums that the digital revolution has made possible. This may prove to create as radical a change in the relationship between people and the institutions of society as did the invention of movable type – the Gutenberg Revolution. The parallels are dramatic. Movable type and the printing press almost instantly eliminated the laborious hand copying of documents; the church and the state lost control over what people could know, making democracy technologically possible for the first time since the Greek city-state.

With the digital revolution, we no longer can say "freedom of the press belongs to those who can afford one."No longer is it just the major institutions of society that are able to disseminate information; now, virtually anyone with a computer can. But as with the Gutenberg Revolution, far greater responsibilities descend upon the public. People must be far more alert and critical in assessing the information provided them because virtually any incompetent or dishonest fool can create a Web site.

Medium-specific distinctions are disappearing, altering how news and information organizations operate. There are very few journalists these days whose work appears in only one medium. W&L grad Mike Allen, who covers the White House for the Washington Post, files stories not just for the paper's 9 p.m. deadline but also throughout the day for the Post's Web site. He appears on streaming video clips on the Web site and on television talk shows. Bloomberg reporters are expected to produce stories in five different media formats. NPR recently produced an archaeological series that included expanded information on its Web site and related specials on the Discovery Channel. As these examples indicate, the digital revolution radically changes the "skills set" that journalists must have today, it multiplies the relationships that journalists have with their audiences, and it changes in fundamental ways how journalists need to think about informing people. Deadlines become constant, because information can appear at any moment on a Web site.

Volume or story length is no longer a constraint, because space on an Internet server is virtually limitless. If video or audio or narrative or graphics or even extensive spreadsheets are needed to best tell the story, all these are available. In other words, journalists may now create a story in whatever ways best tell it, and they can create several different stories for the several different audiences who they hope will want to learn about that topic. And the institutions of society must begin to recognize that people have available vast amounts of information with which to assess them.

The digital revolution, then, frees journalists from the constraints of a single medium and likely will be seen to cause journalists to focus more attention on their audiences, on how to explain what is happening, on what form of information can best tell this story. Related to this is the "hyperlink" nature of the Internet, permitting virtually random roaming by its users – a radical departure from the analog world of linear thought processes.

So, for the journalist, convergence means entirely different ways of thinking about how to convey information. For the public, it means much more information is available from sources of every conceivable stripe, but it requires a far more critical perspective because the veracity of information sources can no longer be taken for granted.

In other words, a revolution in relationships between the institutions of society and people much like the one half a millennium ago that, by making possible the Reformation and Renaissance, transformed the world. This indicates the challenges we in journalism education face. We must learn to embrace the digital revolution and to make our students comfortable with a radical new technology that brings with it dramatic changes in social relationships and different ways of gaining and communicating knowledge.

History of Communications Revolution

When Alexander Graham Bell invented the telephone in 1876, he soon realized that to be a success and genuinely revolutionize the way humans communicate the system would have to work over long distance, or run the risk of remaining little more than an interesting gadgets for academics to mull over. So it did not take him long to improve the range. In that notable twelve months it was extended from around 8 miles to a distance of 143 miles at year's end. But that was still not going to be enough if the telephone was ever going to replace the telegraph. This had already been a part of society for some time, and had gone transcontinental fifteen years previously to take over the primary role of urgent message delivery in the United States from the famous Pony Express, which had been the best bet for speed before then.

Two years later, in 1878 the telephone concept received an extra boost by the installation of the first at the White House by the new President Rutherford B. Hayes; and the first call was between the President and Bell himself, (though some rumor at an earlier and unauthorized use). It always helps to get the Federal Government onside after all, but still, true long distance was some way off and would come to pass in many incremental stages, being powered by new associated inventions and the better application of available technology.

In New York in 1885 the American Telephone and Telegraph Company (AT&T) was incorporated. At this time it was a subsidiary of the American Bell Telephone Company, but was fourteen years later to buy out the assets of its' parent and itself to become the parent of the Bell Telephone System.

Alexander Graham Bell was himself one of the co-founders, and its corporate charter was clear in emphasizing the future importance of long distance telephony: "Connect one or more points in each and every city, town or place in the state of New York with one or more points in every other city, town or place in said state and in each and every other of the United States, Canada and Mexico; and each and every of said cities, towns and places is to be connected with each and every other city, town or place in said states and countries, and also by cable and other appropriate means with the rest of the known world."

The first long distance step took a line from New York to Philadelphia in 1886, just one year after the company's foundation, and by 1892 the longest line in length stood 950 odd miles between New York and Chicago. This record would hold for a while, as the limits of technology had been reached. An invention called Loading Coils (which were tightly strung copper coils wound up on a coil of iron, and positioned around every mile along the cable they were connected to) and the use of thinner telephone wires helped to extend the distance out further to Denver. But after about 1000 to 1500 miles telephone calls were extremely difficult, there being too much loss of signal for a voice to carry to a receiver clearly.

So consequently the dream of coast-to-coast conversations was 'put on hold'. This sparked up again in 1906 when private inventor Dr. Lee De Forest came up with the three-element-vacuum tube, also know as the audion. This was not fully utilized however until six years later in 1912, when AT&T who had been unsuccessfully attempting to build a similar device themselves, bought the patent from De Forest and began to improve the design by increasing the vacuum of the chamber and lessening the amount of internal gasses, allowing it to be used as a practical amplifier.

Now the way was clear for more progress and on June 17, 1914 at the town of Wendover, Utah; the last pole went up to link the east and west lines and enable the first transcontinental telephone call to be made on January 25 1915. The delay in dates here bizarrely was for public relation reasons, so as to allow the official opening to coincide with the exposition due to be held in San Francisco that year, which was to celebrate the finishing of construction of the Panama Canal.

It was the world's longest telephone line with over two-and-a-half thousand tons of copper wire being strung on near to

130,000 poles. Three of the new vacuum tubes were in place to act as boosters and make the magic work. As well as dignitaries in New York, including Alexander Graham Bell, and San Francisco, also taking part in the inaugural transcontinental call was the U.S. President of the day Woodrow Wilson, in Washington D.C. and from Jekyll Island, Georgia, the AT&T President, Theodore Vail.

Now long distance would really take off, with increased demand from the populace leading to more innovation. Underground cables would carry greater number of wires and a new 'carrier-current' system was developed. This way of doing things could send multiple calls down a single pair of wires by differing the frequencies of voices, rather than transmitting them at their natural level. The first of these carriers was hooked up between Baltimore and Pittsburgh in 1918, the same year that saw the ending of World War One.

In the roaring twenties things marched ahead again with technical and administrative improvements to switchboards making it easier for the operators to use, and quicker for the callers to get their calls. No longer would so large a string of operators be needed along the route of a single call, each looking up pathways through enormous route books to connect the circuit correctly to progress the call. Average completion times plummeted to around a couple of minutes waiting time from above seven minutes. Also in the twenties the phone lines were used by newspapers to transmit and receive wire photographs via a very basic form of facsimile machine (fax). A sight well known and loved from classic movies, when newspaper reporters were often heroes of the plot.

In the forties and fifties automation speeded things up again for long distance with now only a single operator needed to route a call. Routing information codes used by the operators were superceded with area codes seen by all today. These were first used as operator shortcuts dialed into the new switches which the machines could then translate into the lengthy data it needed. Now the call-completion times dropped to less than 20 seconds. When computers came later, the caller themselves could use the codes on their phones with direct dialing, waiting times were slashed to 1 to 2 seconds and operators were no longer needed, apart from enquiries work.

Back to the lines themselves and 1929 saw the invention of co-axial cable (co-ax) which was the original broadband. This was first used experimentally by AT&T in 1936 between New York and Philadelphia. It proved successful and began to be used regularly in 1941. This original was known as L1 and had the capacity to deal with 480 phone calls at once.

Co-axial cable was half of the next generation, its partner for long distance being microwave radio relay.

Radio-telephones had already been around for some time but were limited in use and reliability, microwaves were far superior; although since 1927 a commercial long distance service had existed between the Unites States and the United Kingdom. A joint venture of these nations which would later evolve to include Canada, South Africa, Kenya, Australia and Egypt as well as ships afar in the oceans. The U.S. transmitter being sited in Deal, New Jersey. This link with England would continue until 1956 when a transatlantic co-axial cable system was laid at the cost of 42 million dollars. An enormous sum in those days, but the project was a resounding success until becoming obsolete at the hands of satellites, and soon began paying for itself.

Co-ax could do this alone, but for land, especially across awkward geographical features, the microwave relay had the advantages of relative cheapness of installation and lower maintenance cost. It began in the United States in 1947, sending long distance calls along a series of seven towers between New

York and Boston. This original system was very effective but later ones could carry an eight-fold increase in telephone conversations. So it wasn't long, (just eight years in fact) before a transcontinental microwave radio relay system with a-hundred-and-seven towers linked up New York again with San Francisco for the cost of 40 million dollars.

By 1958 microwave relays accounted for 25% of the United States' long distance calls, and by the end of the 1970s this had risen to 70%, with co-ax dealing with the remainder.

Long distance calling cards made their debut in Europe in 1975, but these early versions were prepaid swipe cards which could only be used via special pay-phones. They grew in circulation slowly around the world and the U.S. but the introduction of PIN numbers, allowing them to be made use of with any phone would later explode their numbers.

The 1980s brought fiber-optics with the first long distance route being installed between the nation's capital and New York in '83. They rapidly took over the communications world, leading to total nationwide coverage by the end of that decade.

These thin, and now super-thin, glass fibers which send digital data by rapid pulses of light could probably not have been dreamed of by Alexander Graham Bell in 1876, but have transformed the audio clarity of the long distance phone calls that had their wheels set in motion by him all those years ago.

Ironically, as this latest technology seemed to complete the AT&T mission, a year after their introduction the company was broken up for anti-monopoly reasons, leading to the many hundreds of long distance carriers that serve the consumers today.

Television is undergoing its biggest change since its invention more than half a century ago - bigger even than the introduction of colour pictures in the 1960s and the arrival of multichannel satellite TV in the late 1980s. The new generation of digital televisions use the same technology as computers - anything a PC can do a digital TV can do as well. No longer an example of a passive "lean back" technology - enjoyed with minimum effort and engagement while slumped on the couch - the digital TV is an active "lean forward" device, designed for interaction and involvement.

Digital TVs invite you to play games, to seek out on-screen information and entertainment and to part with your money in ways old-style broadcasters never even dreamed of. But no one knows how long this digital revolution will take to sweep away the old analogue television world, or how profound its impact will be on our viewing habits, our pockets and the broadcasting industry.

Global media companies and governments alike are fumbling in the dark, while huge sums are invested in a technology whose appeal to viewers and consumers remains unproven. More than a third of British homes now have digital TVs, or set-top boxes which convert digital signals into something a conventional TV can make sense of. Of these, 5.7 million subscribe to the service delivered via satellite by Sky TV, controlled by Rupert Murdoch, whose other UK interests include the Times and Sunday Times, Sun and News of the World.

Sky Digital's rapid growth in the three and a half years since it launched has been achieved partly by converting existing analogue customers to digital and partly by generous subsidies. Set-top boxes costing around £200 to manufacture are supplied free - there is a modest installation fee - provided customers agree to connect the box to a BT phone line. Viewers can then make use of interactive services, offered by both the BBC and Sky on news and sport programmes. The interactive benefits include extra information on-screen using the remote control, or alternative camera angles during sports events, and e-commerce facilities.

Digital TV requires a satellite dish, set-top box or new TV set. Just over 1.25m households subscribe to the service provided by now-collapsed ITV Digital, delivered to conventional rooftop television aerials from conventional earthbound transmitters.

ITV Digital was jointly owned by Granada and Carlton Communications, the two companies which between them control the majority of the ITV network. They used their muscle within ITV to rename the old OnDigital service last year.

ITV Digital's channels are mostly supplied by Sky and its interactive service, ITV Active, also allows access to the internet. Customers can also get the ITV Sport Channel - which is absent from the Sky service. ITV1 itself only appeared on Sky for the first time late last year.

But as Sky Digital grew, and as viewing to mainstream channels like ITV1 and BBC One fell disproportionately fast in digital homes, the policy was rethought. Now ITV Digital has gone into administration - the ITV Sport Channel failed to pick up enough subscribers to justify the £315m three-year deal it signed to cover the Nationwide League. Despite this, a £100 set-top box offering access to all free digital channels - such as BBC Four, CBBC, CBeebies and ITV2 - should be in the shops shortly.

The UK's two main cable companies, NTL and Telewest Broadband, claim 1.14m and 641,000 customers apiece. They too offer Sky's package of channels, plus services like "video on demand" (where the viewer pays to watch a film which can be paused, rewound or fast-forwarded just like a video) not available on Sky or ITV Digital. The companies are able to offer this because cable networks can carry much more data much faster than phone lines. But the launch and growth of digital cable services has not all been plain sailing.

It has been hampered by technical glitches and by the persistent failure of UK cable companies to get their marketing and customer service right, despite their undoubted technological superiority. Both companies are saddled with big debts as well.

Future of Communication Technologies

Electronic production and delivery of information open vast opportunities for the traditional media as well as for their new competitors. Old ideas about the appropriate role of the media will have to be adjusted accordingly. Until now, mass communications has been defined as the industrialised production, reproduction, and multiple distribution of messages through technological devices. The focus has been on information products produced in a relatively few centralised locations and distributed through separate one-way channels to large groups of consumers. The new technologies change this. The telephone system becomes something else, used increasingly for nonvoice transmissions between information machines rather than for person-to-person conversations.

Media resources are being reassembled in a new pattern, consisting of three main parts. The first consists of the traditional mass media; these will remain for many years the most important element in the pattern in terms of their reach and influence. The second consists of the advanced electronic mass media; this part of the pattern operates primarily within the new information utility, competing increasingly with older media services. Finally, there is the emergence of newer forms of personal electronic media, formed by clusters of like-minded people in order to fulfil their own professional or individual information needs. First, the traditional media-broadcast TV, film, radio, and print. Collectively, they are a formidable presence, with annual revenues of over $ 100 billion in the United States. These services will continue to expand, particularly in international markets.

Media industries are facing up to the need for change in the ways they produce and distribute their wares. It is not just a question of marketing old products in new ways. Increasingly, the content and purpose of the products themselves are changing. The second part of the new media pattern involves electronic mass communications services: consumer data banks, multimedia computers, and so forth.

Electronic production and distribution of information are still focused primarily on the needs of large organisations, public and private. Within a decade, however, the mass consumeri-sation of computer-based information and entertainment resources will become a commonplace fact. The transition has been slow in coming, early ventures in the field having been bedevilled by inadequate technology and consumer resistance, both of which are now being overcome. The first computer-literate generation is already moving into the media marketplace. They are men and women who are at ease with keyboards, data disks, and video monitors. Their skills, learned in schools and offices, are now being transferred home. Consumer data services such as Prodigy and CompuServe, using ordinary telephone lines, are following.

Over three million homes now subscribe to these services, not as exotic innovations but as useful, taken- for-granted aids to daily living. The next step consists of multimedia capabilities, combining data, sound, and video services in one electronic package. These services will be delivered to multimedia PCs or to telecomputers, the replacements for today's TV sets, with large, high-definition screens that are better adapted to entertainment programs. Such machines will be standard fixtures in most US homes early in the next century, providing services from traditional media organisations as well as from their new electronic competitors.

Finally, we are seeing the emergence of personal electronic media as a new form of mass communications. A small but important example is the 50,000 electronic bulletin boards now available to computer owners throughout the United States. The most spectacular example of mass networking is the Internet, a network of networks. Internet is a high- speed data communications grid linking over 10,000 other networks, private and public, around the globe. Originally developed by the US government for communications between domestic research institutes, Internet has blossomed into the world's largest data facility, with an estimated 10 million users. Internet and other data highways have turned small computers into electronic meeting places. Once the playtoys of small groups of computer buffs, bulletin boards are now available to millions of people. Exchanges of information are still made mainly by videotext.

In the next few years, the range of capabilities of these networks will expand to video and sound as a new generation of multimedia computers becomes available. Computer bulletin boards and similar developments are an electronic extension of a long tradition of 'small media' that have always operated around the fringes of the larger media services. The small media include amateur and citizen-band radio grids, facsimile networks, and the vast range of special interest newsletters, magazines, and bulletins serving, collectively, tens of millions of people. These traditional small-media outlets will continue, but they will be supplemented, and perhaps eventually be replaced, by the new computer-based alternatives.

Increasingly the new personal networks are taking on the characteristics of traditional mass media. These networks serve, collectively, large audiences with specific information needs, from the frivolous to the profound. They also spur the trend toward the fractionalisation of mass audiences, which has been characteristic of the media in recent decades. Electronic bulletin boards are only part of this restructuring of media resources. The new personal networks also include networking by touch-tone and cellular phones, audio and video cassettes, personal fax machines, small-group satellite conferencing, and low-powered television transmitters designed to serve specialised audiences. Some of these technologies may fall by the wayside, as they are replace by more efficient methods. It will be years before their total impact can be adequate measured given the innovative, unpredictable ways they are used by individual groups, from nuclear disarmament activists to stamp collectors.

Personal electronic networking is a present-day reality, and it is changing the information habits of millions of people. Only when we chuck conventional idea about the media can we recognise that these networks are a new form of mass communications, providing decentralised, inter-active information resources that expand and often take the place of traditional mass media services. Whole telecommu-nities are being formed around these new resources.

In a society dedicated to the extension of the market-place of ideas, we have no choice but to accept the social risks of the new personal electronic networks. The tele-communications industry is already restructuring its facilities to serve this new market, making it easier to form individualised networks. Electronic mail and other networking arrangements are an everyday fact of life.

A breakthrough occurred in 1991 when the MCI telephone network began marketing its Friends and Family service, which offered greatly reduced rates to individuals who wanted to form their own personalised network. The company signed up five million customers within a few months. It takes no great stretch of the imagination to see this voice service extended to data and video networking over the company's fibre-optic network. Another service, scheduled for activation in the mid-1990s, may be a major channel for personal electronic networks. It is called Interactive Video Data Service (IVDS), authorised by the FCC in 1992. IVDS permits viewers to use their regular television set for interactive video links with a variety of resources, from home shopping services to educational courses. Although promoted primarily as a business marketing device, IVDS may also be used to develop consumer information and entertainment services that compete with more conventional media.

The marketplace is still a useful indicator of social needs. However valuable a new product or service may appear to be, it does not become a viable choice until a seller puts a price on its value and a significant number of buyers agree. The new media services are no exception to that process.Marketplace economics will thus be a major force in determining the shape and purposes of the new mass communications structure. Market-driven decisions in the past have helped to create in the United States the most varied, open communications system in the world. In the coming years, new technologies can extend that system to a truly universal multimedia information utility.

The restructuring of communications channels will bring kaleidoscopic changes in the media, both the traditional sectors and their new electronic competitors. The transition to this new media environment will not be easy. Most of the old guidelines are being smudged or even wiped out. Media managers face difficult decisions on the pace at which they will adapt to technological changes. The temptation to stick with old products and practices will be strong. It will be reinforced by the resistance that consumers have put up against adopting many of the new electronic services.

Surveys of cable TV subscribers over the years have

shown that most viewers limit themselves to five or six channels. The idea of 150 channels, now being installed in many cable systems, leaves them nonplussed. Moreover, many of the new technologies involve more expense for both media providers and consumers. Television and videocassettes gained almost instant consumer acceptance in past years because they were relatively cheap, were easy to use, and delivered a recognisable, attractive service. Mass adoption of the new electronic services is proving to be much slower. Meanwhile, the media industries must deal with more immediate problems. These include the fragmentation of their traditional audiences, in part because of changing national demographics. Population growth in the coming decade will take place overwhelmingly within the African-American, Hispanic, and Asian communities.

These industries also face the well- documented erosion of their audience among younger age groups, particularly in the film, newspaper, and magazine sectors. This trend began in the 1960s with the generation whose ideas a interests were formed by Vietnam, Woodstock, and other symbols of alienation. The media industries assumed that the disaffection was temporary and that younger people would 'come home' to the older information outlets in due course. With some exceptions, this has not happened. The media audience erosion continues, particularly among news outlets.

In the publications sector, multimedia conglomerates have had only sporadic success in developing synergies between their print products and their other holdings. Large newspaper and magazine firms have focused primarily on buying other publications, resulting in so-called chain ownership. The traditional argument against chain ownership has been that it discourages diversity of news and editor opinion at the local level. However, increases in one-newspaper towns cannot be blamed exclusively on the increase in chain ownership. Another reason is the well-documented decrease in total US newspaper readership. Twenty-five years ago, ABC, NBC, and CBS controlled, through direct ownership or affiliation, almost all local stations. They also produced the major share of prime-time entertainment programming. Both of these advantages have been seriously eroded in recent years.

The production of and the profits from prime-time entertainment programmes are now centred in the Hollywood studios, following an FCC decision that effectively eliminated network ownership of these shows. Local station affiliates are operating more independently of the networks. Cable TV has cut deeply into broadcast television's audience base. There is also new competition from a fourth network, Fox Television, and from the rapid increase in the number of independent stations. The outcome has been a greater quantity, although not necessarily a better quality, of broadcast television programming at both the national and local levels. In the area of cable television, the trend toward conglomeratisation is striking. Here, a half dozen companies control most local cable networks under virtually monopolistic conditions. These conglomerates also have effective control over the most popular cable programming, particularly satellite-delivered services such as HBO, Showtime, and the sports networks. They have, moreover, tried to use this control to exclude competing programme providers. This oligopolistic situation poses a serious threat to media competition and diversity.

The threat is heightened as the major cable companies move aggressively to supply hundreds of channels of multi-media services to US homes and other consumer locations. Under circumstances of normal competition, such extended services would be a welcome development, contributing to greater diversity of information and entertainment. The circumstances are not, however, normal. Cable conglo-merates have lobbied hard to preserve their control over local networks and the programme services they supply. The big film studios controlled most Hollywood production, as well as the major theater chains through which their films were distributed. In television, ABC, CBS, and NBC had similar control over network programming and their affiliated local station outlets. The industry-wide vertical integration in films and television severely restricted outside competition. This did not change until the federal government stepped in under the antitrust laws, forcing the big studios to sell off their theatre holdings. In television, the big three networks were required to open programme acquisition to outside producers.

Although the cable TV industry's control over both programmes and distribution outlets is similar to earlier experiences with films and television, there is an important difference. Vertical integration of production and distri-bution in films and television involved, in each case, a single media product. However, the cable industry's hold on vertical integration takes in all major media—film, tele-vision, radio, and print—which can be delivered electro-nically to homes and other consumer locations through high-capacity lines.

The mass media have an important mediating role to play both in documenting the new realities and in providing a forum for discussing them. Will the new media services accept that role, so necessary to our individual and collective survival in the new post-industrial environment? There are powerful forces, inside and outside the industry, favouring greater trivialisation of information. 'Infotainment' is the buzzword among media producers and advertising executives these days as they grapple with the problem of retaining their audiences in highly competitive markets. Gresham's Law, defining how the bad drives out the good, operates as readily in the media business as in any other. These issues are part of the larger question concerning how advanced information technologies can change the ways we see ourselves and how we relate to the world around us. We communicate primarily to tell stories. These stories both reflect and re-form our self-images and our communal values.

For most of human history, stories were told by storytellers to small groups of listeners, gathered in a village square or by a fireside. It is only in the past 500 years that the role of the storyteller has begun to be replaced by a machine-produced resource—the printed book. Now we are moving into the age of image communications—first photography, then film and television, and now multimedia computing. These resources deliver powerful messages to enormously expanded audiences. Battered by their drumbeat pervasiveness, the defences against them begin to break down. The result, too often, is a loss of the purposes and interconnectedness by which we were sustained—personally and as a community.

3

Development of Broad-band Audiovisual Services

The advent of digital communcation technologies have produced a plethora of innovative interactive multimedia services and created a new distribution platform for audio and visual content and information. Today, the broadband audio-visual services has enabled telecommunications operators to offer services that had previously been restricted to broadcasters. These services will provide an incentive to increase the speed of broadband connections because high speed is necessary in order to ensure the quality of programming. They will also encourage new investment in broadband infrastructure and accelerate the uptake of broadband in households.

Digital interactive broadband audio-visual services are in particular bringing broadband telecommunications and television broadcasting closer together. Using high-speed Internet for broadcasting, online services, such as video-on-demand (VOD) and live streaming, is generating a new market. Broadband audio-visual services can also expand accessibility to content, by which it might even increase traditional television audiences. There has been a shift in the role of Internet from a text medium to 'broadcasting' for audio-visual information and entertainment, both over the traditional television and the Internet.

Broadband audio-visual services have emerged by means of development of convergence and thus can be a good model to consider the impact and implications of convergence in ICT sectors. It is not easy to predict with certainty the way in which broadband telecommunications and broadcasting will converge and what the impact of this will be on consumer behaviour. However, there are sound arguments to support a review of existing policy and regulatory frameworks to take into account the trend in convergence and to ensure that new services can grow.

A number of countries, however, have set targets for digitalisation. In Austria, for example, digital television will have completely replaced analogue signals by 2012. In Japan, digitalisation of terrestrial television will start in December 2003 and it is expected to be completed by 2011. Indeed, some other countries have dramatically increased the coverage and sales of digital television in recent years. The United States is a leader in this area, and there are 1 230 stations in at least 192 television markets transmitting a digital signal as of September 2003. Factory-to-dealer sales of digital television products in the United States in 2002 totalled 2 487 502 units and USD 4.2 billion, which surpassed 2001 sales by 73% in volume and 61% in revenue terms.

This 'digital revolution' not only expands the number of channels carried on traditional over-theair broadcast but also enables the delivery of a variety of content, some of which was only seen in the telecommunications arena previously. While terrestrial digital television may compete directly with broadband audio-visual services, it also allows for sharing a variety of digital content between different platforms.

The term "broadband audio-visual services" is used here to refer to a group of services that deliver content to users via high speed Internet access. In this context, the history of broadband audiovisual services is not a long one. While it has been said that radio took 30 years and television took 13 years to reach an audience of 50 million, Internet seems to have achieved this threshold within only a few years. It was in 1995 that the first audio was streamed over the Internet.

Early pioneers of audio-visual service over the Internet did not expect audio developments to be as rapid since the network at that time, initially developed for the military, was not meant to be a broadcast medium. Another initial problem was the fact that most users of this service had to make a contract with companies to deliver the content with a limited amount of bandwidth.

Due to the short supply of bandwidth, initial providers of the service had to consider the solution to shorten the time to download the content over a telephone line. Some companies tried to establish their own software as the best way for users to view audio-visual broadcasts or multimedia files on the Internet.

Three main factors helped to substantially ameliorate the situation:

— development of broadband Internet access,

— digitalisation, and

— Internet Protocol technology.

The development of broadband Internet access with increasing access speeds, together with innovation of appropriate software, has been the most significant factor encouraging innovation of broadband audio-visual services. Broadband audio-visual services involve 'streaming media' technology, which is a means of delivering motion and sound from the source to the receiving end.

Streaming media technology makes it possible to deliver multimedia files including audio and video over the Internet. Using this technology requires an Internet connection of at least 30 Kbps, and often more to ensure the reception of streamed content. This requirement is provided by broadband Internet access. However, it is necessary to obtain speeds of 10-100 Mbps to establish subscription-based business models on broadband audiovisual service.

With the increasing deployment of high-speed broadband networks, users have been able to gain access to a variety of digital programmes not only over terrestrial broadcast but also over broadband networks including ADSL, satellite, and cable.

Recently there has been progress in enhancing the speed of broadband networks in some OECD countries, especially through the deployment of fibre-optic cable networks that allow much faster speeds than DSL networks. There are approximately 70 consumer fibre access networks operating in the United States as of March 2003. A study estimates that total fibre-to-the-home subscribers will reach 315 000 by the end of 2003.In Japan, NTT East is planning to cover 80% of households passed by fibre-to-the-home networks by the end of 2004, providing speeds between 10-100 Mbps to customers.In Korea, Hanaro Telecom has deployed fibre-optic cable networks covering about 100 cities by the end of 2002.In Iceland, Iceland Telecom (Siminn) is deploying fibre-optic cable networks across the country.

Since broadband audio-visual services are far from mature in terms of market penetration, further development in broadband market supported by deployment of broadband infrastructure is necessary before the full effects of new developments have an impact.

In this regard, some optimistic estimation might demonstrate the future growth of broadband audio-visual services: Estimates predict that the European broadband market will expand at an annual rate of 68% over the next few years and be worth USD 18.9 billion in 2006. These estimates foresee that a total of 41 million households will be connected via all high-speed Internet services by the end of 2006.

The digitalisation of content distribution is one of the most influential developments impacting on broadcasting in recent years. While many of the radio and television programmes are based on analogue transmissions in most OECD countries, the conversion to digital transmission is taking place. In Sweden, for example, digital terrestrial television first started in 1999 and has already reached 90% penetration as of March 2003. The Swedish parliament decided in May 2003 that the switch over to digital television will be completed by February 2008.In Australia, digital television broadcasting began in major cities in January 2001 and will be extended to regional stations by 2004.In the United Kingdom, digital television penetration is estimated to have increased to 41.4% of households at the end of 2002.In the near future, digital television will be the main distribution standard.

Some OECD countries are actively trying to increase the penetration of digital television. For instance, Germany is seeking to address relatively poor digital television penetration rates through calls for 15 federal media authorities to create a joint digitalisation fund to finance a nationwide roll-out of digital television.A study predicts that there will be a worldwide total of 96.7 million households with access to digital television by the end of 2003.

Digitalisation will bring better picture quality as well as high-quality sound to television. The number of channels will increase up to 100 times including twice the current number of over-the-air services. More importantly, digitalisation is changing the way radio and television programmes are produced and distributed.

Digitalisation enables convergence between telecommunications and broadcasting by allowing the same content produced for the Internet to be used for digital broadcasting services.

In other words, the recent development of digital technology has paved the way for the use of common infrastructures for broadcasting and telecommunications. It also allows such services as pay-per-view or pay-per-channel for customer. Given that a number of broadband audio-visual services are adopting pay-per-view type programmes, this feature will increase competition between over-the-air broadcasting and broadband audio-visual services. Currently, however, digital television still serves a very limited market and suffers from a lack of suitable standardisation, even though cable and satellite digital television is rapidly expanding in some countries. Hence efforts towards convergence by allowing a combination of television sets and Internet access terminals have not yet proven very suitable for users.

The development of Internet Protocol (IP) technology has given an impetus to the development of high-speed broadband audio-visual service. Unlike conventional audio-visual services over the Internet, which deliver programmes on a point-to-point basis, IP Multicast technology has enabled service providers to reach mass audiences at lower costs. This technology sends out the signal to several domains of Internet Service Providers (ISPs) simultaneously, allowing the distribution of audio content over the Internet to a mass audience while substantially lowering distribution costs.

Applications that take advantage of IP multicast include videoconferencing, distance learning, and distribution of live news. The problem remains, however, that the vast majority of Internet routers installed during the late 1990s do not support this IP multicast protocol. For the future, the 'next generation' Internet is expected to enhance the quality of broadband audiovisual services. In particular, Internet protocol Version 6 (IPv6) technology designed by the Internet Engineering Task Force (IETF) may contribute to further progress of broadcasting over the Internet. IPv6 is expected to add a number of improvements to IPv4 in areas such as routing and network configuration.

IPv6 has more affinity with IP Multicast technology and would facilitate upgrading the quality of broadband audio-visual services in two dimensions. First, the function of multicast is installed as a default in IPv6, through which the same content can easily be provided to a large audience at the same time. Second, it ensures quality of service in telecommunications with a configuration in which data communication has a lower priority whereas voice or image has a higher priority. A number of projects using IPv6 are currently ongoing. In the European Union, for example, a three-year project called 6NET, started early 2002, plans to deploy pan-European IPv6 backbone infrastructure stimulating European research and industry to play a leading role in next generation Internet.

Broadband audio-visual services provide audio and video content via high-speed Internet access. There are several ways to categorise these services. From the perspective of what is delivered on the Internet, broadband Internet radio (audio) and broadband Internet television (video) are two different forms.

Digital audio content delivery specifies a system for the transmission of high quality audio via a digital radio channel. It is especially designed for wireless broadband Internet. Broadband Internet radio will be able to rival terrestrial radio in delivering better than CD quality sound to worldwide audiences at competitive rates.

Digital video content delivery is another type of service, which is based on streaming technologies for the transmission of video and synchronised audio content.

In terms of content delivery mechanisms, there are two

types of broadband audio-visual services:

— the first is the download type that plays the audio and video content after they have been downloaded to the customer's terminal;

— the second is through streaming which delivers the data without waiting for viewers' terminals to download all the data.

The majority of current broadband audio-visual services rely on streaming technology.

Streaming type broadband audio-visual services can be divided into two categories: live services and archived services represented by video-on-demand (VOD). Live streaming media enables delivering highprofile content to a global audience, such as over-the-air television. Video or audio file is encoded live at the server and delivered instantly over the Internet according to a pre-determined schedule by the provider.

Live services are mainly used for such applications as concerts and sports. On-demand streaming media are not limited to particular times and can be viewed by users at their convenience. The stream is recorded and hosted on a media server so that the user can gain access anytime. Archived services are mainly used for news and weather forecasting programmes. While it places a large load on networks, access by users could be distributed to different time zones.

Focusing on streaming technologies themselves, broadband audio-visual services include both basic streaming and advanced streaming. Basic streaming simply makes audio and video available through the Internet. This is almost the same as television or radio except that the content is coming over the Internet.

Advanced streaming adds more features to enrich the

experience for both user and presenter. With advanced streaming, for example, it will be possible for providers to track users, which will provide useful information to meet user requirements and compete. It also enables pay-per-view content by accepting and processing credit cards for payment. Furthermore, it allows audiences to communicate interactively with the presenter during a live content delivery. This categorisation will lead to classification between 'supplement-type content delivery' and 'original-type content delivery.'

Supplement-type content delivery refers to broadband audio-visual services which deliver programmes as a replacement for over-the-air programmes. Original-type content delivery means that the applications used in the broadband audio-visual services are specially designed for Internet, not for the replacement of the terrestrial programmes, e.g. business communications. It is also possible to classify broadband visual services into subscription-based content and free content.

The former is represented by pay-per-view content delivery where viewers pay for access to programmes. Basically, the service is charged separately from a basic Internet subscription. Free content is often supported by advertising. With regard to broadband audio services, subscription-based type services are not yet common. However, live pay-per-view streams of sporting events have become a way to gain profit from broadband audio-visual services.

Applications of Broadband Audio-visual Services

Broadband audio-visual services use existing technology at both the service provider and customer sites, and create a wider market without significant investment in equipment. This aspect has two implications. First, the ability of the Internet to provide an unlimited number of information channels for users, which are more than those of traditional broadcasting. In addition, broadband audio-visual services provide a way to deliver real-time information, which can be easily downloaded, to a group of users.

As an entrepreneurial management solution, broadband audio-visual services can also be an effective tool to lower costs of delivering information and administering selected programmes. Second, broadband audiovisual services provide a way to take advantage of market interest within a subscriber base. For the service providers, broadband audio-visual services can be a means to use extra channels and available bandwidth to generate revenue through new services.

For consumers, broadband audio-visual service would be attractive in that delivery of content on live events in real time over the Internet can be offered without a television set. With streaming technologies, audio and video content can be available for viewers at their convenience without being downloaded.

In addition, as the coverage of broadband audio-visual services is global with virtually no channel limitations, content can be available from any of the millions of host sites over the Internet unless the programme is a subscription-based one. Consumers can also enjoy interactivity, such as participation in programmes.

Consumer Benefits

Traditionally, broadband audio-visual services have enabled users to obtain some increased benefits in comparison with over-the-air broadcasting as represented by the following examples. However, these advantages are now available with digital broadcasting which is linked to the Internet.

(a) *A programme overview*: Users will be able to access a

guide to offer an overview of programmes. The guide will be an easy means to navigate between programmes.

(b) *Background Information*: Users will be able to view background information relative to programmes. This information will remain accessible for the whole programme.

(c) *Information search*: Users will be able to search for more information on the Internet in addition to the background information search.

(d)*News flashes*: Users will be able to receive news flashes and other real-time information while watching a programme.

(e) *Programme interactivity*: The programmes over the Internet can be interactive. For example, users will be able to vote in programme polls.

From the ISP business perspective broadband audio-visual services enable the use of accumulated web-log information at the server for marketing information for products and services.It is also easy to monitor responses from users by making the most of the internet's interactivity. From the content providers' point of view, broadband audio-visual services can be a great promotional tool.

According to Arbitron, for example, online music fans who listen to Internet radio programmes on a weekly basis buy 21 CDs each year in the United States compared to 13 CDs for other consumers. Apple has a business model to offer music online to broadband users based on a pay-per-track model instead of subscriptions with low costs (USD 0.99 per track).

From the advertisers' point of view, broadband audio-visual services provide an effective pipeline to deliver their message to a targeted audience with reduced costs and without time constraints. In addition, unlike television commercial messages, advertising in broadband audio-visual services can easily target consumers taking into account their specific tastes.

It is also possible to update advertising information quickly as well as to collect questionnaires from consumers, which enables easy processing of information owing to the interactivity.

One indication that broadband audio-visual services are growing in popularity is the fact that more than 100 000 copies of free streaming players are downloaded over the Internet daily.Broadband audiovisual service is growing as a tool for training, events, conferences, news and instant delivery of corporate messages as well.

Some examples of content over broadband audio-visual services are given below:

(a) News

— Part of the news broadcast on the television is re-broadcast on the Internet.

— Newspaper publishing companies provide news on the Internet with videos.

(b) Films

— Broadband audio-visual service is used as an opportunity of giving a preview or the first run of a film.

— Film show with audience participation is provided on the Internet.

(c) Entertainment

— Broadband audio-visual service is used to promote well-known entertainers.

— Programmes of local broadcasting companies are broadcast live on the Internet.

(d) Sports

— Live broadcast of a sports game can be made either free or by pay-per-view.

(e) Education

— Internet broadcast of live seminars or conferences.

(f) Business

— Broadband audio-visual service is used as an advertisement of the providers' own services and products.

(g) Music

— Live broadcast of a concert is broadcast over the Internet.

— Broadband audio-visual service is used for promotion of music designed for online sales.

(h) Others

— Discussions in Parliament are broadcast on the Internet.

At present broadband audio-visual services are still at the development stage rather than replacing over-the-air broadcasting. But, because of the trend in convergence between Internet and traditional broadcasting, it is important to review the differences between the two in order to understand the implications of broadband audio-visual services on regulatory policy as well as on the market.

The first difference concerns regulations on market entry. While traditional over-the-air broadcasting has a number of regulatory 'barriers' to meet for market entry, in particular the requirement to obtain a licence, media ownership issues and direct regulation of content (programming quality and range etc.), broadband audio-visual services are not constrained by any entry obligations.

Since most of the regulatory obligations on over-the-air broadcasting derive from controls of the radio spectrum as well as political and cultural requirements, broadband audio-visual services are essentially free from these obligations. For traditional over-the-air broadcasting markets the limited spectrum made available and consequently the limited number of licences issued has meant that there is limited market competition in most countries.

At the same time, it is increasingly salient in some countries that whether broadband audio-visual services are constrained or not by entry regulations depends on the way in which they are delivered to the user more than on the platform on which they are delivered. In Italy, for example, providers of broadband audio-visual services would require a licence if the services are delivered on a programming basis in which the user is merely passive and may not freely select the programme or the timing, irrespective of the platform.

The second difference is in terms of cost structure. While over-the-air broadcasting generally has high fixed costs and low variable costs, broadband audio-visual services have much lower fixed and variable costs. It means that the financial barriers to market entry are relatively low in the case of broadband audiovisual services. Apart from the investment in the deployment of broadband networks and transmission costs, broadband audio-visual services need relatively limited capital resources. In many cases, however, audio-visual content such as music or video content requires copyright permission and incurs copyright payments and this may change the economics of service provision.

The third difference is the proportion of penetration. While almost all households currently have a television set and use terrestrial television frequently in most OECD countries, use of broadband audio-visual service is still limited. The relatively low penetration rate in broadband Internet access, except in the case of Korea, means that broadband audio-visual services are still far from universally on a par with terrestrial television.

The fourth difference is in terms of the structure of the services. Over-the-air television broadcasting, whether it is analogue or digital transmission, is fundamentally a one-way delivery of programmes to an audience. On the other hand, broadband audio-visual services, whether download or streaming, were originally a point-to-point communication (often called uni-cast) using Internet protocol, even though they have increasingly become similar to 'broadcasting' with the development of IP multicast technology. Therefore, broadband audio-visual services are inherently interactive and not subject to any 'programming' whereas traditional over-the-air broadcasting essentially follows a programmed schedule of presentations, over which users have no control. This feature might imply that broadband audio-visual services will not reduce new kinds of over-the-air broadcasting services.

The fifth difference is the number of channels. In most OECD countries, there are currently only a few channels in over-the-air broadcasting for analogue TV, each of which can show one programme at one time for a mass audience. Broadband audio-visual services are not limited by the number of channels. They are usually provided on the basis of the concept of a 'library', which will imply a higher degree of control by the user. However, digitalisation of over-the-air broadcasting has the potential to dramatically change the number of channels.

Digital broadcasting can create 'server-type broadcasting', which enables viewers to search for specific programmes or scenes they wish to watch by using electronic programming guides (EPG). It is also possible to search the hard discs of other servers connected to the Internet if the target programme is not on the hard disc of the viewer's server.

In Japan, for example, the legal framework has been formulated by the government in order to allow for the introduction of server-type broadcasting to all digital broadcasting. Thus, digital broadcasting will allow a user to view a programme at a convenient time, a function similar to that available to broadband audio-visual services.

A further difference would be the fact that broadband audio-visual services are different from both broadcasting and telecommunications services in the way intellectual property rights are managed and protected. This has profound implications on the business model of broadband audio-visual services.

Broadband Audio-Visual Services Market

Broadband audio-visual services are becoming a key part of the ICT industry. The demand for streaming video is in particular growing. Research shows that among broadband users 34% are thought to stream video from the Internet and 31% to download it.Behind this fact, there have been gradual shifts from both the telecommunication and broadcasting sides to the market side of broadband audio-visual service. This would be an example of convergence between telecommunications and broadcasting services.

The mutual entering between the two industries is, in some cases, being made from both sides rather than by 'invading' the other field directly by gathering in a 'grey zone', *i.e.* broadband audio-visual service,. This reflects the reality of convergence and the difficulty of assigning firms to boxes such as 'telecommunications operators' and 'broadcasters.' In this context, convergence is a diversification process in the broadband communications arena rather than a simple unification process of the traditionally separated telecommunications and broadcasting sectors.

With the increase in bandwidth, a number of telecommunications operators are entering into the market for broadband audio-visual services. In comparison with entry into the broadcasting market, in which there are scarce resources (spectrum frequencies) and high entry barriers, it is much easier for telecommunications operators to enter the market of broadband audio-visual services.

A major motivation for market entry is to expand their revenue base, in particular to increase average revenue per customer, and to maintain their existing customers. By bundling telephony, broadband Internet access and programming services (broadband audio-visual services) together, telecommunication operators can provide a comprehensive package of services to their customers, and benefit from economies of scope.

Broadband audio-visual services are becoming an important way not only to attract new customers but also to retain existing customers since it is likely that customer churn will be reduced if a customer is subscribing to voice, Internet access and content services from a single supplier. Such bundling of services often results in lower prices for consumers compared to subscribing to separate services.

A number of enterprises are offering integrated services, often by finding strategic partners. In Italy, for example, Fastweb, a fibre-optic cable provider, launched integrated television on-demand, high-speed Internet and telephony services and in October 2001 reached an agreement with TELE+, an Italian pay-TV company, to deliver film and sport from TELE+ using its fibre television.Another possible motivation for market entry seemingly comes from their desire to enhance their brand names.

With provision of value-added services, telecommunications operators can show that they are leading and competitive companies in the field of broadband communication. The fact that a number of companies initiated 'free' broadband audio-visual services such as Internet radio stations, which are not necessarily aimed at reaching wider audiences, is an example.

There are some examples of market entry by telecommunications operators in OECD countries, which sometimes takes place in the form of strategic partnerships with broadcasting or content creating companies. In the United Kingdom, for example, BT Openworld, the broadband content arm of British Telecom (BT), moved into broadband audio-visual services in November 2002 by creating a new sports channel called Sportal OnDemand in partnership with other companies.

The provision of this channel will enable broadband subscribers in the United Kingdom to watch a wide range of VOD sports programming covering major sports events worldwide.In Japan, NTT East began to broadcast Internet radio programmes experimentally with streaming delivery system from December 2002 to March 2003.NTT is also planning to launch a new service during 2003, which delivers programmes of the terrestrial and satellite television companies via its fibre-optic networks.

A satellite broadcasting company Sky PerfecTV and Japan's public broadcasting company NHK are showing their interests to use this plan. For NHK which has an obligation of universal programme provision by law, this kind of service is expected to play a complementary role to cover local areas where radio signal is difficult to reach.KDDI also announced in May 2003 that it would launch broadband audio-visual services using fibre-optic networks during 2003.

In Spain, a telecommunications operator Auna is offering integrated services of television, telephony and Internet by using its broadband network.Auna also announced in March 2003 that it would incorporate interactive middleware and products of OpenTV, interactive television company, in order to provide new interactive services. In June 2003, the incumbent operator Telefonica signed an agreement with Kreatel Communications, a provider of solutions for TV-centric services in IP networks, to launch TV and video services over ADSL.

In Austria, the incumbent Telekom Austria launched a new broadband audio-visual service in June 2003, which allows AonSpeed users to receive live broadcasts via the Internet.Telecommunications operators have tended to give priority to video-type services, but there has been an increasing emphasis on broadband audio service as well.

In the United Kingdom, for example, British Telecom (BT) launched a range of broadband-related products in March 2003, which include a portable radio that can be used anywhere in the house and allows users to tune in to a number of Internet radio stations. It is likely that this service will be bundled with a BT Internet connection based on BT's strategy to stimulate demand for access to its broadband networks.

Entering the broadband audio-visual service market has been a strategy for some ISPs as well. Since broadband users tend to expect a variety of attractive services that narrowband users can not enjoy, provision of broadband audio-visual services may be necessary to avoid losing customers by offering them exclusive information and entertainment. For example, America Online (AOL) began to offer high-speed free access to CNN's video news services to its subscribers in February 2003.This collaboration reflects their business plan to hold on to Internet users switching to broadband from dial-up connections by offering them exclusive audio-visual information.

Loudeye Corp., a leading digital media service provider, announced new versions of broadband audio-visual service applications designed to meet the growing demand for broadband audio-visual services across vertical markets including training, marketing, and corporate communications in November 2002.BellSouth, Internet (DSL) service provider, entered into an agreement with Movielink, an online movie download service provider, in August 2003 to offer its DSL users a customised version of Movielink's movie rental service.

In Japan, Japan's Softbank Corp (Yahoo BB) started to provide television service on its ADSL network. Users of this service will pay a monthly fee of USD 21.35 for a basic package in addition to an ADSL subscription fee.

In the United Kingdom, the first internet-only television channel, which is only available via broadband networks or ISDN, was launched by Worldart Media Television in October 2002.Like some telecommunications operators, there are some ISPs who are broadening the types of their services. For example, Loudeye launched Loudeye Radio V2.0, which includes a plug-and-play encoder and P2P streaming, in order to provide a broadband audio-visual service solution to terrestrial radio channels in September 2002. Some ISPs are putting stress on corporate broadband audio-visual service, targeting at corporate communications.

Corporate communications broadcasts to individual employees and consumers could be one of the most profitable areas of broadband audio-visual services as well as digital television services. An increasing numbers of corporations are discovering that broadband audio-visual service is a powerful and cost-effective way to communicate with employees and customers, especially with those who do not always have time to attend company events. For example, Corporate Communications Broadcast Network (CCBN) has been offering broadcasting on the Internet for communications between companies and investment community.

Convergence by over-the-air broadcasters is also taking place via the Internet market. Providing broadband audio-visual services can be a good target for them to approach the telecommunications market and to expand the variety of services. This type of market entry is viewed as supplementing existing services rather than replacing them. It can be expected that terrestrial broadcasting, as some analysts argue, will remain an important sector providing important services to the society it serves.

Broadcasters in the Internet broadcast audio-visual market are either providing the same content over broadband as that provided on terrestrial broadcasting, such as live concert shows, or they are providing the same content but in an enhanced way, such as archived news on the Internet. In some cases broadcast content is specific to broadband audio-visual services.

It is increasingly salient that broadcasters are seeking to offer combined services with broadband. As one example, in the United Kingdom satellite broadcaster BSkyB is looking at introducing a broadband Internet access package to rival cable network operators such as NTL and Telewest. In addition to this broadband offering, BSkyB is also planning to introduce a broadband-enabled digital set-top box to enhance its interactive digital television services.In some OECD countries, an increasing numbers of over-the-air television broadcasters are getting into the market for broadband audio-visual services. In the United States, for example, large broadcasting companies such as NBC, ABC News, and CNN, started providing limited broadband audio-visual services as early as the late 1990s. Among these, ABC television network, a subsidiary of Walt Disney Co., plans to launch a 24-hour news service that will be available to subscribers to the existing ABC News on Demand broadband service.

In the Netherlands, Dutch television broadcaster SBS6

decided to start broadcasting parallel versions of some of its popular programmes on the Internet in December 2002.

In the United Kingdom, the BBC, which has operated broadband audio-visual service as well, launched a new Website in January 2003 that enables browsers to access past BBC news reports in the form of video or audio, which can drawn from archived media.

In France, a national broadcaster, TF1, is to test broadband television services over a six month trial in Paris. This test involves 200 users receiving TV and video, together with high-speed Internet access, over broadband networks.

Another project of TF1 is called 'Dream TV', which encompasses 200 households located in Boulogne Billancourt and in the 15arrondissement of Paris who can receive an array of 24 television channels over ADSL networks.

However, it appears that broadcasters in some countries lag behind telecommunications operators in entering broadband audio-visual service markets. This may be because the incentive for broadcasting operators to enter the market is primarily motivated by the will to keep the market under control instead of favouring its growth. In addition, for many of the above examples, companies are setting-up different departments so that there is little institutional convergence taking place. For example, there is often different editorial responsibility for Internet and over-the-air television.

There has been some criticism of over-the-air public broadcasters for their broadband audio-visual service trials. In Germany, for example, a private broadcasting company, VPRT, criticised public broadcasters who tried to increase their online activities. This criticism was particularly aimed at a deal between the public channel ZDF and Internet service provider T-Online, which enabled Internet users to watch the news service Heute on a special common Heute/T-Online site.

In Japan, NHK, the Japanese public broadcasting company, was criticised by private broadcasters as well as the newspaper industry when it announced commencement of a form of broadband audio-visual services in January 2000.The complaint was based on the argument that broadband audio-visual services by NHK would hamper private activities even if the programmes were 'recycled' ones (*i.e.* already broadcast on terrestrial television/radio).

It is important to differentiate between services offered which are equivalent to free over-the-air broadcasting and those offered which are equivalent to pay-TV. For the over-the-air broadcasting arena, it has traditionally been recognised that consumers can receive their television programme for free at the point of consumption. However, with the proliferation of cable television a myriad of new television channels gave broadcasters in some countries, such as the United States, more power as gatekeepers of content. As a consequence, an increasing number of people are willing to pay for television in these countries. Providers of broadband audio-visual services, who originally focused on free broadcasting, have increasingly turned toward offering pay-TV type Internet broadcasting.

Operators of a pay-TV type services will be able to offer a more comprehensive range of programming including popular movies and sport. In some OECD countries such as the United States, pay- TV seems to be flourishing in recent years. However, some providers of pay-TV type services are facing some difficulties due to high programming cost and the difficulty of accessing high-quality content. This situation encourages them to form new partnerships or create joint ventures.

The acquisition of Italian pay-TV operator Telepiu Spa and Stream Spa by an Australian company News Corporation

Limited, approved by the European Commission in April 2003, is an example in line with this direction.Market entry by cable television broadcasters Cable television broadcasters differ from over-the-air broadcasters in terms of entry into the market of broadband audio-visual services. They already provide a wide range of programming and often provide access to high-speed broadband Internet services as well as digital content over their systems.

Thus, they have less motivation than over-the-air broadcasters to enter the market. It is possible over time that the distinction between traditional programming and content they provide over their broadband service would blur. With increasing competition from DSL in the broadband Internet access market, however, a number of cable television companies will find provision of broadband audio-visual services via cable an appropriate means to keep their customers, as is the case of traditional telecommunications operators.

In addition, as broadband telephony services develop it can be expected that many cable companies will begin offering telephony, broadband, and programming, as a package to attract customers. In Japan, for example, a cable television company Jupiter Telecommunications Co., which also operates J-COM Broadband, is offering CATV programming, telephony and broadband services as a package with a reduction rate within certain areas.In the United States, the merger between AT&T and Comcast was decided by the FCC in November 2002, and the newly formed AT&T Comcast, as the largest cable company in that country, will offer a combined service including CATV, telephony, and broadband Internet.

There have also been trials in the market for broadband audio-visual services from other industries in recent years. The most relevant example would be market entry from the software industry and content providers that are taking advantage of relatively low entry costs. In the United States, for example, in March 2003 Microsoft began a service that lets users with broadband Internet access send live video to each other at rates as high as 15 frames per second, which approaches the quality of television.

Yahoo has been involved in corporate broadband audio-visual services since acquiring Broadcast.com in 1999 and launched a new broadband audio-visual service that lets companies produce their own multimedia events in April 2002.Yahoo also launched a broadband audio-visual service named Yahoo Platinum in March 2003.

One of the main marketing features for this service is the deal which Yahoo has signed with the annual National Collegiate Athletic Association (NCAA) college basketball competition in the United States, where early games will be broadcast over the Internet.

In France, a software company called Nexedi launched an Internet-based system called TVBrick that will allow connection with TV and with the Internet via a broadband link in June 2003.This system is targeted at Japanese people overseas who want to keep up with their favourite TV shows on the broadband Internet.

In Spain, a provider of adult entertainment services Private Media Group announced in January 2003 that it would offer high-quality VOD services on its broadband audio-visual site.

In Japan, Sony, jointly with Sony Communication Network, began to offer a broadband audio-visual service called So-Net Broadband Mega-Channel to registered subscribers in February 2002. The content covers movie, music, sports, shopping, and live drama. Sony foresees that Internet and television will merge in the future and that television will be reborn as a digital entertainment centre in the home.Market entry from an industry which is not directly relevant to broadband audio-visual services is also increasing.

In the Netherlands, for example, Jamby, a Dutch online entertainment company, began testing out two Internet television sites in August 2001. The aim of the experimental sites was to interest advertisers in new online methods of entertainment.

In the United Kingdom, EMI Record Music, a division of U.K.EMI Group, launched an online streaming music service with Streamwaves, an Internetbased subscription music provider, in November 2000.Matching Hat, a magazine publisher, also launched a new interactive financial information service distributed over the Internet and TV-on-demand in May 2001. Its 'Your Money Interactive Television' offers 40 kinds of three-minute streaming video clips about specialised personal finance subjects.

In France, a French regional newspaper, Ouest-France, was to launch a local Internet television service named Maville TV in July 2002 despite the failure of Internet television at a national level.Some mass-media companies strategically use broadband audio-visual services to extend their customer reach. For example, Reuters, the financial news group, started to launch a streaming video service ranging in March 2003 providing news video clips for free aimed at extending its coverage from financial to consumer content.

With the growth of the broadband audio-visual service market, a large number of mergers or alliances were being formed at various levels in recent years. This is one of the by-products of convergence, and corporate strategy appears to be aimed at finding a strategic partner rather than at vertical integration. This relates to the reality that many markets have rules which constrain some kinds of alliances.

For example, rules and laws sometimes require separation between telecommunications operators and cable operators. In addition, it is often the case with the countries that there are ownership rules which apply and might constrain some alliances. Depending on the market, these types of rules may be the reason to promote the trend of strategic partnerships.

A typical type of partnership is between ISPs and broadcasters. In the United Kingdom, for example, AOL teamed up with BSkyB to provide Sky Digital's subscribers with increased interactive TV functionality. BBC Worldwide will create Internet-based programming for the RealNetworks service to the US market after a deal is signed between the two companies.

In Ireland, Hitouch entered into a strategic partnership with Interactive1 and they will set up a joint venture called WebChannels to provide video and audio broadband audio-visual services.

In Japan, Yahoo BB announced in April 2003 that it would enter into a partnership with a private broadcaster, Fuji Television, and offer video programmes of Fuji News Network (FNN) free. While broadband audio-visual service provided by Yahoo BB had previously been restricted to its ADSL subscribers, this new service will enable other users to view the programmes with special software.

Mergers are also taking place between ISPs and content providers. In the United States, for example, the merger between AOL and Time Warner approved by the FCC in January 2001 has combined AOL's far-reaching Internet audience with Time Warner's vast entertainment content.

Telecommunications operators are also giving increasing attention to strategic partnerships with broadcasters, especially pay-TV companies, in order to position themselves in content markets.In Australia, for example, Telstra sought to bundle its telephony service with Foxtel's subscription-based television service. Under this deal Telstra offers Foxtel's pay-TV services at a discount rate to retail residential users who also buy fixed line telephony services from Telstra. While there was some opposition to this alliance on competition grounds, the regulator ACCC decided not to intervene on this deal in November 2002.

In Japan, NTT Broadband Initiative (NTT-BB) began to offer FNN news programmes of Fuji Television to subscribers of its broadband network BROBA in April 2003.Cross-industrial collaboration is also active.

In the United States, for example, the Consumer Financial Network (CFN), a leading provider of financial and life planning solutions, and Internet Broadcasting Systems (IBS) announced a major joint marketing initiative in June 2000. IBS provides CFN's YouDecide.com with prominent placement throughout their local broadband audio-visual service channels, while also promoting the services of YouDecide.com on television through IBS-affiliated television stations.At the same time, the development of alliances among broadband audio-visual service providers is also a growing trend.

In Europe, for example, a major European Information Society Technology (IST) project, SAMBITS, was launched in January 2000 to bring together key broadcasters, researchers, academics and industrialists across Europe to drive convergence based on broadband audio-visual services.A group represented by some of the major DSL providers announced in March 2003 that they would develop, standardise and support an open model for interactive entertainment services over broadband DSL. The initiating group consists of Alcatel, Belgacom, Philips Consumer Electronics, Bluewin/Swisscom, Telecom Italia, Telefonica, Telecom Austria and Thomson.

In the United States, major broadband audio-visual service providers had a new forum in October 2002 with the launch of the Webcaster Alliance following the legislation of HR. 5469 (Small Webcasters Amendment Act).

With the growing numbers of partnerships, some conflict of interest between service providers sometimes occurs. For example, Echostar Communications Corp., a satellite television provider, filed a lawsuit against Microsoft-owned WebTV Networks, alleging that the company neglected their collaborative relationship and built equipment for rival operator DirecTV. If these movements of organising alliances go through a consolidation process, they need to be examined by the relevant antitrust authorities who may impose conditions on the operation if a dominant position is strengthened. Alternatively, if there is no consolidation process, the incumbent telecommunications operators are still bound by regulatory requirements in relation to their traditional markets (voice and data) which ensure a level playing field among players.

Problems of Broadband Audio-visual Services

The emergence of broadband audio-visual services is raising some problems. The first is to ensure that revenues can be generated to support a business. Without advertising revenues, free access to broadband content cannot be sustained unless supported by other paying services.

There is a need for all the players involved in the industry, including content providers, to find an appropriate business model. Quality could also be a problem unless sufficient bandwidth is delivered in that, unlike traditional television, it seems more likely that broadband audio-visual services cannot at present maintain a sufficient level of high quality especially for images. The failure to deliver a constant level of service can slow diffusion and lose customers. In order to enhance the quality, higher network bandwidth is required. There is also a 'high bandwidth problem'.

At present broadband telecommunications is characterised

by asymmetric communications that is high data rates downstream to subscribers but relatively low data rates upstream from subscribers. In broadband audio-visual service, however, symmetric communications are often required to support interactivity. Further development of broadband Internet networks may in certain cases be a precondition for growth of the broadband audio-visual service market.

Nevertheless, recent progress in broadband audio-visual service technologies has substantially benefited broadband audio-visual service providers. In the area of audio compression technologies, for example, RealNetworks and Microsoft each have made strides in providing the same quality sound in smaller packages. RealNetwork's new technology has reduced file sizes by 30% while keeping the same sound quality, and Microsoft's test version of Windows Media 9 released in September 2002 offered a 20% gain over its previous version. These smaller file sizes lead directly to lower costs as broadband audio-visual service providers are paying to send less bits over the broadband network

.Some broadband audio-visual sites adopted this high-quality image. For example, Major League Baseball (MLB) will use compression schemes from RealNetworks that give users a full-screen picture, which is better than VHS quality at a streaming rate.Another problem is allegedly insufficient user-friendliness.

Normally, each audience must have a media player (format) downloaded and installed on his or her own computer in order to receive broadband audio-visual service programmes. In addition, the media player must be compatible with the format used by the broadband audio-visual service providers. This lack of standardisation can also slow growth although there are now only a handful of popular options including Real Player, MPEG, Shock Wave, Windows Media Player, and Quick Time.

Interoperability between different standards should also be ensured, and thus competing, open and industry-led interoperable systems should be agreed upon. Additionally, it will be important to develop user-friendly terminals so that anyone can easily gain access to programming on broadband Internet.

A further problem is intellectual property rights represented by copyright. Since digital content is very easy to copy, copyright issues have become extremely important for the broadband audio-visual service industry. Business models may only be adopted by the industry if policy addresses the issue of copyright by balancing the interests of all the stakeholders involved.

The copyright problem is associated with issues of online distribution of content. Broadband audio-visual services should be based on commercially viable distribution models that take into consideration and adequately remunerate all segments of the value chain in a networked environment.

Examples of software to view broadband audio-visual services are given below:

(a) *RealPlayer:* Developed by RealNetworks Inc., it enables access to image and sound in real time. It comes pre-installed on many computers and the Mac and Windows versions can be downloaded for free.

(b) *MPEG*: Developed by Moving Picture Experts Group, it is used for coding audio-visual information in a digital compressed format. A number of MPEG players are available for Macintosh and Windows platforms, most of which are free.

(c) *Shock Wave:* Developed by Macromedia Inc., it enables users to watch animation, entertainment, and interactive multimedia.

(d) *Windows Media Player:* Developed by Microsoft, plays

music and video and has roughly the equivalent quality as RealPlayer. It is bundled with Microsoft's Internet Explorer Web browser.

(e) *QuickTime:* Developed by Apple Computer, it was one of the first widespread digital-video technologies and enables playing and editing of a variety of media including images, sound, and virtual reality. It is given away free of charge and is bundled with all Macintosh computers and some Windows PCs.

The present conjuncture in the telecommunication industry relative to intellectual property rights is having a great impact on market growth for broadband audio-visual services resulting in some service providers exiting the market. The number of broadband audio-visual service channels as of September 2002 was estimated at about 4 000, significantly lower than the 5 700 stations in 2001.In the year 2001 alone, the number of broadband audio service providers reportedly declined by 31%, with US stations accounting for the major steep decline. Some of these closures resulted from threats to take action against copyright infringement where Internet radio stations were playing music without paying copyright. Over 1,000 US stations and Internet-only broadband audio-visual service providers reportedly quit streaming online in 2001.For example, in June 2002 Yahoo decided to close down several of its broadcast services including FinanceVision and Yahoo Radio because of the continual 'lacklustre' performance.

Broadband audio-visual service can be a potential way of bypassing the existing regulatory frameworks of broadcasting such as licence and content regulations. This is because it is technologically possible for broadband audio-visual service providers to download terrestrial television signals and to re-transmit them via their broadband networks.

In Canada, for example, iCraveTV streamed the programming of US broadcast TV stations online 24 hours a day without receiving permission from broadcasters or copyright holders in 1999. Although the Internet is not regulated in Canada the legal position of iCraveTV was not clear. A number of US programmers filed a lawsuit against iCraveTV and the company decide to shut down the service. Also in Canada JumpTV wanted to re-transmit over-the-air television signals in 2002.

In Canada cable TV companies have the right to retransmit over-the-air signals by paying an appropriate copyright fee. JumpTV wanted the same right as CATV companies using broadband. Their initiative led to a change in the Canadian Copyright Act and JumpTV was given, subject to paying an appropriate copyright fee, permission to retransmit signals. However, they also needed to guarantee that only Canadian users would have access to the content they retransmitted.

Although JumpTV decide not to develop their service and withdrew from the market, their case helped in laying the policy groundwork for potential new market entrants in the provision of broadband Internet video services in order not to leak the content out of the country. While JumpTV claim to make sure that online visitors are coming exclusively from Canada, it would be difficult to find out to what extent the border-control technology works. They point out that their act is legally admitted under compulsory licensing law in Canada that prescribes companies can re-transmit any television broadcast on the air.If these movements increase in the future, regulators might be obliged to further loosen the existing regulations.

Although broadband audio-visual services have the potential to increase competition by providing a new platform for programming, there is also the possibility that they decrease competition if major companies in the industry offer bundled services which include broadband audio-visual and telephony.

Business Models

The uncertainty as to the future profitability of the broadband audio-visual service industry, linked for a large part to the question of copyright fees, is holding back market entry by many companies. In the Netherlands, for example, XS4ALL, a Dutch ISP, is taking a 'wait and see' approach. In 2002, about 15 000 subscribers to XS4ALL's broadband service participated in the Dutch ISP's six-week trial in Internet television broadcasting. In spite of an enthusiastic response, XS4ALL is analysing the results from this experiment before deciding its next move.

The DSL-TV Foundation, which was set up by some Internet service providers, is to begin broadcasting six international channels via the Internet for free in a trial of broadband audio-visual service in March 2003, which can only be viewed by users in the Netherlands. Yet, it has currently no plans to commercially offer broadband television services.

The issue of new business models for broadband audio-visual services should be addressed mainly by the industry based on the concept of a new form of distribution in a networked environment with high levels of usage and low costs of distribution. One of the keys to create a steady business model in the field of broadband audio-visual service is content. The increase of broadband Internet users is likely to be content driven, which means that the content broadcast over the Internet should be designed to convince more users that broadband is worth the 'extra money.'

There are some government initiatives to stimulate the development of broadband content among OECD countries, one example is in the United Kingdom. The UK government view is that these initiatives will result in productivity and competitiveness gains both in the content industry and for the wider economy. In 2003, the feasibility study on broadband content pilots, commissioned by the Department of Trade and Industry (DTI), was completed.

The pilots concentrated on business models for broadband content development and their contribution to competitiveness and productivity, both to the UK content industry and to the wider economy. The study made a strong case that the pilots represented a significant opportunity for UK business, and that the DTI and industry should take them forward. The report included a full evaluation of the rationale of each pilot together with a recommendation on the proposed structure for the pilots and implementation plan.

Two of the AKC recommendations are directed towards helping SMEs enhance their productivity and competitiveness through the use of broadband content. These are:

— Developing broadband marketing to provide consumers with compelling broadband experiences, initially within the Tourism industry.

— Making tools available for more effective collaborative working within a creative industries cluster.

Another project called the Broadband Channel would involve creating a central body commissioning high quality broadband content for access by distributors. It is different in nature and size from the other projects and is more of a market maker than a pilot. However, some argue that there is currently no 'killer application' in broadband Internet access.In terms of content delivery, there already exist a number of rival media such as over-the-air TV, satellite, and cable broadcasting as well as rental video, DVD, and CD. The one area where broadband has an advantage over other media is the ability to obtain information content on demand and access to archive content.

There are basically two types of potential business models for online content delivery. One model is advertising-based relying solely on revenue from advertisements without levying subscription fees, and another type is subscription-based levying a fee for content use from subscribers. In addition, there could be a pay-per-view model for broadband audio-visual services on different platforms.

This model can exist by itself without a subscription and service providers can favour this kind of model in the future in order to sell their services outside their subscription customer base and thereby extend their market share.

Given that traditional broadcasting is in many countries supported by advertisements and that the likelihood of higher advertisement budgets is small, the future of broadband audio-visual services may be on a subscription-based or pay-per-view business model providing personalised content linked with the opportunity for interactivity. In this context, it is noteworthy that some broadband audio-visual service providers have sought to improve upon terrestrial broadcasting business by increasing interactive elements, such as to rate songs, or to participate in contests. With regard to MTV, a worldwide broadband audio-visual service company, for example, interactive application has enabled MTV viewers to vote for their favourite stars before and during the MTV Europe Music Awards.

A potentially profitable content targeted at specific groups would be sports coverage. Broadband audio-visual services currently account for only about 1% of sports industry revenues and most of it is either recent highlights or archived material, since the rights to the content are either not available or held by over-the-air television broadcasters. Nevertheless, some estimates predict that this rate is set to grow as sports rights holders begin to support emerging channels more actively.

A variety of business models being tested in recent years would demonstrate this estimate. For example, Major League

Baseball (MLB) and RealOne are said to be the most successful examples of subscription-based services, with 1 000 users paying up to USD 14.95 per month for access to archived material.

In an effort to attract viewers, some companies are also seeking to make then Internet-only content and services available via television. In Germany, for example, T-Online is planning to offer customers such services as video-on-demand and an electronic programme guide starting in late 2003. A special settop box, connecting the television, the antenna cable and broadband provider, will be required to access the package.

Some broadband audio-visual service providers are increasing the number of subscription-based programmes. For example, the United Kingdom-based 'Ministry of Sound' announced in February 2003 that it would begin to offer subscription-based online content. The company is reportedly planning to create an interactive community on the Internet where radio and video broadcasting are combined with chat rooms allowing users to interact with each other on a pay-per-track basis.In addition, the economics of concurrent video streams in terms of the business model would be highlighted in the wake of the development of broadband audio-visual services. For example:

— Hosting and distribution costs for broadband content items can be 100-1 000 times higher than that for an equivalent number of narrowband text and graphics content.

— There is a markedly different business model for broadband content between a public and private broadcaster, and the associated geographical implications for access.

— Issues of the geography of users versus rights management need to be addressed. For example, a question can be raised as to whether it is right that an Australian who pays no license fee or UK tax can watch video streams for free while costing the UK taxpayer.

— The scalable, affordable network capacity needs are vast.

The increase in the number of content distribution networks, such as Akamai Technologies and Seedra Networks, has lessened the need for large bandwidth. Furthermore, newer services to distribute content at a lower cost have sprung up in recent years. Instead of using large server infrastructures that handle all user traffic, peer-to-peer content delivery services direct new users to other users that are already hosting a particular piece of content. This is working as a delivery method for content, such as streaming media, at much lower cost and more efficient bandwidth usage. Sound quality is not yet equal to that of traditional content delivery network services.

While peer-to-peer streaming is still in its infancy, some content delivery companies, such as Kontiki or AllCast, have employed this technology.Radio Free Virgin, one of the free broadband audio-visual service providers, was also one of the first to take advantage of peer-to-peer streaming technology. The technology uses individual listeners' computers as relay points so that one listener can draw a stream of music from another listener's PC instead of from central servers. While peer-to-peer technology would not totally replace the content delivery networks, it would be able to replace up to 80% of the traffic for a substantially lower price.

Audiovisual Service Development: Impact on Market

Telecommunications market

Developments in the broadband audio-visual service market can help stimulate the demand for broadband access. In turn, the growth in this market and its potential will help stimulate the deployment of higher speed networks. In a number of OECD countries operators are already upgrading the speed of DSL as well as creating new broadband networks and extending the geographic coverage of high speed networks.

In Belgium, for example, 98% of the population had access to Belgacom's ADSL networks with 3 Mbps speed in December 2002. In the United Kingdom, Telewest, broadband communications and media group, began a trial for a new broadband service in March 2003 by offering free upgrades at a connection speed of 2 Mbps to 1 500 of its customers currently subscribed to its 1 Mbps cable broadband package.BT has reportedly also attempted to test a new broadband project which will provide a 1 Mbps ADSL home connection.

Broadband audio-visual services are also stimulating the mobile telecommunication industry. Some mobile operators are seeking to offer audio-visual broadcasting via high-speed 3G telephones. In Korea, for example, a mobile operator KTF is to start broadcasting television channels direct to 3G mobiles via the CDMA2000 1xEV-DO system.In France, Alcatel and TNO Telecom announced in March 2003 that they launched a technical project with RTV television for the development of 3G/UMTS mobile broadcasting services. They will provide a live television broadcasting service from RTL on mobile handsets, using Alcatel's 3G technology as well as TNO's 3G Internet video gateway.

In Portugal, Vodafone Telecel, together with TV1, enabled their subscribers to watch an entire football game on their mobile phone in March 2003.Technological developments to facilitate mobile operators to provide broadband audio-visual services have grown in recent years. For example, PacketVideo and Musiwave announced in April 2003 that their empowered technologies and services, using PacketVideo pv3 Mobilemedia System software solution, would allow users to easily receive audio-visual content over existing GPRS (2.5G) networks.

In Australia, researchers unveiled a chip that lets mobile users receive high-quality face-to-face video and other streaming media at rates faster than most broadband connections at home in February 2003.Some expect that the chip could compete with wireless LANs, which have been increasingly popular among OECD countries.Broadband audio-visual service is also stimulating telecommunications operators to initiate new types of services. For example, BT (BTopenworld) will begin services to remind viewers of TV shows they wanted to watch via their mobile phones.

Broadcasting Market

Arguments have been made that broadband audio-visual service will not affect the broadcasting market because it has not achieved the universal coverage of traditional television and radio. Yet there is evidence that the growth of broadband audio-visual services has the potential to stimulate market competition in the broadcasting sector from two perspectives: first as an alternative to at-home entertainment and access to information, and second, as a platform providing direct competition.

A report from comScore networks, for example, on Internet usage shows that among 45.1 million adults that have a television set and PC in the same room 47% reported they frequently use the Internet while watching television. Competition for the time of viewers is expected to become important and surveys in several OECD countries have shown that time spent viewing television has declined as more people spend longer periods using the Internet.

Traditional television broadcasters are facing some changes in market structures with the development of broadband audio-visual services. Asynchronous communications, that is the ability to cache information for future access, as opposed to real time broadcasting, is viewed by some as an important way for broadcasters to enhance their existing programming by using Internet technology and bandwidth to increase interactivity with customers.

For example, broadcasters could offer a range of information on broadcast programmes which viewers could access on demand. Such developments would change the way terrestrial broadcasting offers its programming. However, two-way, interactive channels or viewerparticipation- type programmes are likely to increase in the future only if appropriate domestic terminals are available to consumers.

'Web-TV' or Internet via television, which enables users to receive Internet content, including broadcast audio and video over the Internet, via television (or PSTN), has fallen into decline with the growth of broadband audio-visual services. This service was originally developed in 1996 by US-based WebTV Network Inc., which was taken over by Microsoft in August 1997. The development of broadband audio-visual services has enabled users to use Internet and television simultaneously without installing a special television set. However, new types of Web-TV services have emerged recently. For example, Monaco Telecom, in partnership with Alcatel and Moviesystem, launched 'SesameTV', VOD service on television via ADSL.

In Japan, Matsushita Electric Industrial Co. is going to equip all digital television sets provided in Japan with high-speed Internet access by connecting them with broadband networks. It will also launch a service allowing viewers to access the Internet from television sets at home.

The process of digitalisation of terrestrial television, along with the increase in content that can be shared with broadband audio-visual services, is resulting in hybrid like services which may in the longer term result in little differentiation between terrestrial broadcasting and broadband broadcasting. For example, the recent development of 'interactive television', which combines traditional television viewing with the interactivity enjoyed by a telecommunications network, might narrow the scope of broadband audio-visual service activities, although some estimates indicate that interactive television will generate only USD 18 billion for service and application revenues in Europe by 2007.

Broadband audio-visual services may begin a process resulting in the trans-border provision of broadcasting services. In many OECD countries, entry by foreign firms in domestic broadcasting markets is constrained by foreign investment limitations and other licensing limitations.

However, using high speed Internet audio-visual services provision can take place across frontiers. For example, the Norwegian Internet browser developer, Opera, began to provide service to the Japanese digital television market in March 2003. According to Opera, Japanese set-top box manufacturer Plat Communication Components will include the company's system for an interactive television browser in its broadband terminal box, which delivers television over IP networks.

At the same time, it is important to note that the trans-border provision of broadband audio-visual services can result in problems from differences in legal or social norms. An example is the case where Yahoo was ordered by a French court to bar French Internet users from its Websites selling Nazi memorabilia in November 2000.The process of trans-border service provision is most noticeable for broadband radio broadcasting.

Access to Internet radio, and to several stations dedicated to providing specialised music or information, has helped bolster the radio sector and has allowed people from different countries to access a wide range of different cultural and information material. Internet radio has also allowed ethnic minorities and immigrants in those countries that have large immigrant populations to develop their own cultural radio stations. Radio has often been viewed by the music industry as the best way to ensure the success of a new recording. The wider, and global, reach of broadband radio can play a significant role in this regard by allowing global audiences to hear new recordings.

Broadband audio providers have been viewed by some as posing a 'threat' to conventional radio stations. There is a greater variety of programming and versatility in broadband audio service than in conventional radio. Moreover, setting up a broadband audio service operation is cheaper.

Commercial radio stations may have little interest in initiating broadband audio services because the potential to expand their listener base may not add to their revenues. It is also unlikely that there will be much demand for pay-radio. However, many commercial radio stations have set up Internet radio operations and many have allowed access to archived programming through the Internet. This is viewed as a means of consolidating their customer base and competing in their local area for customers while enhancing their brand name.

Broadband audio service has been viewed as a threat to the recording or music industry in some countries such as the United States. While commercial radio and the music industry in general are close partners, the high quality of transmission over the Internet has also been viewed by some as seriously undermining the recording industry's ability to sell recordings.

Recording artists, trade associations and regulatory agencies are continuing to examine the competing interests between the delivery of content and the protection of intellectual property rights in a digital environment. Work is underway to develop appropriate technology and standards for multiple radio platforms to deliver services to mobile, cordless and fixed access users. It will therefore be important for existing commercial radio operations to become familiar with the different technological platforms and be able to offer appropriate content for these platforms.

At the same time, broadband audio-visual service demonstrates how the traditional relationships between service providers and customers have changed. Traditionally, broadcast viewers have been accustomed to access broadcast channels for free or for a fixed fee. Over-the-air broadcasters have had their services financed by advertisements as well as public contributions, while telecommunications services have been charged for access and actual use by subscribers. However, subscription-based programmes and the new business model based on them are likely to increase with the influence of broadband audio-visual services.

Research shows that broadband subscribers are more open to paying for online content than narrowband users. The research found that 25% of broadband users were willing to pay for music compared to 18% of narrowband users whereas 18% of broadband users were willing to pay for movies compared to 11% of narrowband users.Since broadband audio-visual service is fundamentally based on broadband Internet access, this fact might imply that broadband audio-visual service is much easier to attract users to subscription-based broadcasting.

One of the seemingly negative impacts on the broadcasting market is 'dominance' over certain types of broadcasting programmes.Exclusive contracting of popular programming may prevent competing services and broadcasters from gaining access to such valuable content, restricting competition in service provision. In particular, issues surrounding broadband broadcasting of sports have given rise to significant concerns about market competition.

In a number of OECD countries, certain companies make a contract with a major sports team and dominate the right to broadcast the event on the Internet. In Japan, for example, Bitway, provided by Toppan Printing Corporation, began to offer 'Web Stadium HANSHIN Tigers Live' in August 2000, whereby the live game events of a famous Japanese baseball team are delivered on the Internet.

In the United States, MLB Advanced Media began to offer live video and audio webcasts of baseball games in August 2002. Currently, these are limited only to viewers outside their favourite team's television-coverage area. In March 2003, however, MLB Advanced Media announced a paying service allowing baseball fans around the world the ability to watch live full-game broadcasts online of 45 games each week throughout the 2003 season on MLB.com.Exclusive provision of content also occurs in the music arena. For example, ArcoStream, a streaming and webhosting provider, was selected in November 2002 as the service provision partner of RollingStones.com, the official Rolling Stones fan club Website. AcroStream delivers audio and video content from the band's concert tour exclusively.

While advertising is a primary source of revenue for many terrestrial broadcasters, the development of broadband audio-visual service is changing the focus of advertising. Many broadband audio-visual services are trying to target advertising to the specific tastes and interests of individual customers. This tool is gradually being adopted in terrestrial broadcasting as well by some advertising companies.

In Japan, for example, Hakuhodo has developed a new technology to change the content of advertisements according to the taste of viewers. The technology allows advertisers to send several types of commercials in advance to the server and to deliver them to different viewers. Hakuhodo began a trial of this commercial delivery in programmes of a satellite broadcasting company ep Broadcasting Corporation, in March 2003.

The development of broadband audio-visual service also encourages convergence of terminals. Originally broadband audio-visual services were based on a PC platform. In other words, the PC has taken on the function of a television set in this service. Likewise, some television sets can also access the Internet in the wake of the development of broadband audio-visual service. Users will therefore be able to use one terminal to access different platforms to access content.

Cable Television Market

Before the advent of broadband audio-visual service, cable television companies had already established an early lead in offering both high-speed Internet access and television packages. In a number of OECD countries, however, the number of DSL subscribers has surpassed that of cable subscribers, following the unbundling of the local loop.The increase in DSL subscribers relative to cable modems could be viewed as a competitive 'threat' for cable television companies relative to the market positioning of telecommunications operators that are attempting to enter the broadband audio-visual market. Unlike over-the-air television, cable television is not usually accessible without subscription charges.

Broadband audio-visual services that are free or are based on low subscription charges can compete directly with cable television. There is no evidence that this has happened yet given that broadband access is still relatively premature in the majority of OECD countries. However, many CATV companies are trying to compete with telecommunication companies to provide broadband Internet access by increasing bandwidth or through price competition.

As for terrestrial broadcasting, cable companies will also be encouraged to implement digitalisation by the development of broadband audio-visual services. A study predicts that digital cable will increase from 28.6 million by the end of 2002 to 37.3 million by the end of 2003.The cable television industry has started over the last few years to develop VOD services.

It has been suggested that VOD via cable television rather than Internet is seen in the industry as more practical and user-friendly, because the cable infrastructure is already in place and its implementation simply requires the deployment of updated set-top boxes and server equipment. Another argument suggests that subscription-based VOD has been identified as the most important short-term factor in developing revenue streams for cable television companies. Some research findings predict that the market of subscription- based VOD via cable television will grow from USD 293 million in 2003 to USD 1.4 billion in 2007.Worldwide cable-based VOD subscribers are expected to grow from just over 3 million regular users at the beginning of 2003 to more than 11 million by 2006.In the United States, for example, Time Warner Cable is offering up to 100 digitised 'movies on demand' and 'subscription video on demand' services to about half a million digital cable subscribers.

Online gaming via cable television might possibly be another focus of the cable industry. In the United Kingdom, for example, the former managing director of Telewest urged the cable industry to move forward in making online gaming attractive to the masses in March 2003. He also contended that a flat-rate charge for CATV would be ultimately unsustainable with the growing popularity of data intensive services such as streaming media.In the same vein, a cable company, NTL, announced in March 2003 that its broadband service would support Xbox gamers who want to use Microsoft's multiplayer online gaming service, Xbox

Live.

Broadband Audio-visual Services: Impact on Regulations

Since the progress of convergence will change the landscape of many traditional media and telecommunications businesses, the development of broadband audio-visual services might lead to regulatory uncertainty which may inhibit investment. It is important to ensure that regulatory frameworks do not hamper the development of broadband audio-visual services and that private investment in this field is not hindered by regulatory frameworks.

One example of the recent improvement of regulatory frameworks in light of the development of broadband audio-visual services is Japan's new law (Laws Concerning Broadcast on Telecommunications Services) implemented in January 2002, which allows broadcasters to offer broadcasting services on telecommunications services provided by telecommunications operators. For instance, BB CableTV (former Broadmedia TV) offers multi-channel broadcasting as well as VOD services using ADSL provided by Yahoo BB to Yahoo BB's subscribers in the wake of the implementation of this law.

One of the major concerns in the regulation of broadband audio-visual services would be that the regulation should ensure technological neutrality between platforms. This neutrality, however, should take into consideration the level of commercial and technical maturity of the different specific platforms.

At the same time, it would be necessary to consider that different converging platforms should not necessarily be subject to different degrees of regulation (for instance, part of the telecommunications world is highly regulated) in a convergent world. Different levels of regulation might hamper the general pace of development of broadband audio-visual services and penalize one platform against another.

Historically, governments often have rules or laws governing ICT industry structure, such as ownership rules for telecommunications as well as for media and general competition and antitrust laws. At the same time, there are also rules or laws governing industry conduct, either on the conduit side or on the content side.

On the conduit side, for example, there may be policies related to transmission of telecommunications, such as those impacting law enforcement, or cable services as well as those related to spectrum. On the content side, in addition to rules specific to cable, satellite and terrestrial television, there are also general copyright and intellectual property right regimes which apply to all types of content. Given that broadband audio-visual services are still in the early stages of development, the policies most likely to be affected are those related to conduct on the content side.

As broadband audio-visual services grow, they may have more impact on the policies related to industry structure. The development of broadband audio-visual services will result in a number of policy challenges in that these services, although in many cases similar to broadcasting services, can be provided on platforms which are not generally regulated. These services are eroding the traditional boundaries between telecommunications and broadcasting, and changing the communications landscape, thus existing regulations may be inappropriate or even harmful to dynamic ICT markets.

Broadband Services and Cable TV Networks

Cable industry is the most successful media enterprise of the past two decades. During the persistent economic recession of the early 1990s, most cable systems and their programme suppliers continued to post increasing profits, unlike many other media businesses. There are already signs that cable TV is entering the ranks of mature industries, with more and more of the aches and pains that institutional maturity brings.

From the double-digit growth of earlier years, single-digit cable TV growth is now projected for the rest of the 1990s. In part, this reflects the fact that cable TV is approaching a saturation point in the number of households it can effectively serve. The cable TV business remains healthy, but the first bloom is off its rose.

A longer-range problem for the industry is represented by the emergence of competition with alternative cable systems and with other technologies. From its beginnings, the cable TV industry has enjoyed monopoly status, through franchises granted by municipalities to its local networks, Now, however, pressure is forcing the renegotiation of many of these franchises so as to allow more competition. In 1992, only about 50 of the industry's 9,400 franchise areas had an alternative cable TV system. That competition will increase as more local franchises are modified to permit other systems. Even more formidable competition may emerge from newer technologies. These include information and entertainment programmes supplied by microwave distribution systems 'wireless cable', by fibre-optic circuits operated by telephone companies, and by transmissions from satellites broadcasting directly into homes.

Although potentially competitive, these technologies are not an immediate threat to cable TV systems. The industry is still riding high, protected in most cases by local monopoly franchises and by its success in supplying a broad array of programme services to subscribers. Cable TV has overcome its closest competition—broadcast television—by becoming the channel through which most people view local and network TV programmes. All this is a long leap from cable's modest beginnings in the 1940s as a retransmitter of over-the-air television stations. Previously, cable subscription rate had been calculated on a single monthly charge for all programmes. With the arrival satellite-delivered services, that billing pattern changed. A 'basic service' charge was made for local television programmes and other advertising-supported channels.

Today the industry is dominated by a handful of companies which are full or partial owners of the local cable systems that provide services most household subscribers. These firms also own, wholly or in part, most of the popular national cable programming services supplied to local systems. Others are diversified communications conglomerates, whose interests oft include publishing, broadcasting, filmmaking, and other media operations.

The cable industry's most formidable potential competitor is the telephone industry, which has long-term plans for wiring all US homes with a high-capacity fibre-optic cable. Fibre links have far greater capabilities than cable TV's present coaxial wires for supplying, among other services. Compression squeezes more capacity into existing wires, allowing present coaxial lines to transmit a hundred or more cable TV channels. The cable industry is betting that increased capacity will satisfy the average subscriber's programming needs for some time to come. Cable operators are also acting to block phone company competition by upgrading many of their systems with fibre cable.

More immediate problems for cable TV include the need to maintain a high level of profitability. The rate of growth is levelling off. The industry continues to have problems with what it calls churn—the persistent turnover in subscribers. Many cable companies also have a heavy debt load, inherited from the high-riding 1980s, when they were expanding their systems, At that time, cable systems were being traded like baseball cards in a schoolyard, often at dizzying prices.

Although the cable industry overall is in good financial shape, it needs to pursue new revenue opportunities. The most immediate increase in revenue will probably come from advertising. Cable advertising has already expanded to the point where subscribers are objecting to 'clutter'—too many commercials interfering with programmes they have already paid for. A 1991 study indicated that cable has significantly more clutter than the television networks in prime time. The cable industry has introduced a new twist in electronic advertising with infomercials, 30-minute advertisements, often masquerading as talk shows that provide viewers with an 800 phone number for ordering the featured products.

Cable system owners worry about consumer acceptance of the new channels, especially consumers' reactions to the inevitable rise in subscriber rates. Over the years, surveys have shown that most cable subscribers limit their viewing to about a half dozen channels. Channel expansion will also spur the adoption of other new services. One of them is digital cable radio, which will do for home stereo what cable has done for TV in a cable radio system, the cable TV wire is split in half. One half is linked, as before, to home TV sets, and the other half is connected to stereo systems.

In recent years cable communications companies have recorded among the highest rates of revenue growth in the communications and information industries segment. Data from the United States Census Bureau show that the cable industry grew by 64% between 1997 and 2001. This compared with 102% for Information Services and Data Processing, 41% for Telecommunications, 31% for publishing, 24% for Motion Picture and Sound Recording and 17% for Television and Radio.

Between 2000 and 2001, cable industry revenues increased by around 15.9% in the United States. These data also indicate strong growth in the provision of cable television and broadband Internet access. The provision of high-speed Internet grew from USD 198 million in 1998 to USD 5.6 billion in 2002. It is interesting to note the pattern of growth and shifts between traditional categories that have been occurring over the last decade. The two areas with strongest growth are wireless service and other revenue which includes Internet access. Substitution between services is readily evident.

Cable television is one of the few platforms for communication where there are more subscribers outside the OECD area than within Member countries. This is a relatively recent occurrence. In 1992, cable subscribers in OECD countries represented 88% of the world's total number of subscribers. A decade later, in 2001, more than 50% of the world's cable subscribers were in non-member countries. China, India and, to a lesser extent, Russia, are responsible for most of these subscribers. By 2000, these countries collectively made up 77% of the cable subscribers outside the OECD area. The availability of cable television ranges from the service not being offered in Greece to nearly 100% coverage in Belgium. While all data are not available, it can be said that cable television is available to more than half the households in OECD countries.

Although complete data are not yet available, there were in excess of 9.2 million cable telephony subscribers at the end of 2002. The available data for 2001 and 2000 were 8 million and 6.7 million respectively. In 2001, the number of lines provided by cable telephony was 1.3% of the total number of fixed lines in OECD countries. This would not have significantly increased in 2002. Although very small in terms of the total market, the impact can be significant in individual markets. In the United Kingdom, for example, some 15.1% of all telephony lines were provided by cable companies. This number takes on added significance in that cable networks only pass around half the total number of households in the United Kingdom. Cable companies in Australia supplied by 5.6% of all lines at the end of 2001. In other markets the overall share of cable telephony is lower but some individual companies are recording very high take-up rates in terms of households passed. It is the latter phenomenon that is providing competitive pressure on telecommunication carriers as they need to respond in those markets where cable telephony service is available. For the future, the cable telephony market is likely to expand but through two different technological platforms.

The majority of cable telephony, to date, has been supplied by cable companies employing copper local loops for business and residential premises alongside their coaxial cable. In the future, it is likely that voice over the internet protocol (VoIP) will come increasingly to the fore. One reason for this is that the number of cable modem connections is growing much faster than the number of cable telephony connections using copper local loops. These cable modem connections will provide the platform for the introduction of VoIP.

In 2003, some cable companies are already offering VoIP and most others are undertaking trials or expect to introduce the service in the near future. VoIP has the potential to grow very quickly if pricing is attractive to users. Consider, for example, that "Yahoo BB!", a Japanese broadband access provider using DSL, signed up 2 million customers in less than 12 months following the launch of commercial service. In the United States VoIP for broadband users ranges from "free" for broadband-to-broadband connections to USD 39.99 for unlimited domestic (and calls to Canada) terminating on a standard telephone line.

The US National Cable and Telecommunications Association (NTCA) believes that with the continued improvements in VoIP, cable-delivered telephone service could evolve into a telecommunications "after thought" of consumers, rather than a separate, independent service. The first signs of this are already evident in the pricing of firms such as "YahooBB!" and Vonage.

The number of cable modem subscribers in the OECD area reached 23 million at the end of 2002. This compared to 30 million DSL subscribers at the same date. The overall number of broadband subscribers in OECD countries was 56 million. This meant that cable modems made up 41% of the overall broadband market, compared with 54% for DSL. Other technologies represented around 3%.

Although cable modem services had an early lead on DSL, the latter overtook the number of cable modem services at the end of 2001. By 2002, the growth rate for DSL was appreciably higher than for cable modems. In that year, the DSL market grew by 83% compared to 53% for cable modem services. In the final quarter of 2002, the pace of DSL increased such that across the OECD the number of DSL subscribers was growing twice as fast as cable. In the EU area, DSL was growing about fives times faster than cable in the final quarter of 2002. By way of contrast, cable modem service was growing faster than DSL in Austria and the United States.

One reason why DSL has overtaken cable modem service is that, in many countries, it is much more widely available. A second factor is that incumbent telecommunication carriers own numerous cable networks. This has had an increasingly negative impact on cable modem growth. That being said, in 2002, the number of cable modem subscribers exceeded that for DSL in 12 OECD countries. The reverse was true in 17 countries, although the difference is negligible in Australia, Hungary and Ireland. In Greece, neither service was available at the end of 2002.

The countries where cable networks significantly outperform DSL, in order of relative magnitude, are the Netherlands, Austria, the United States, Portugal and Canada. Generally this is because of very strong cable performance, but in the case of Portugal there is a very low DSL penetration. On the other hand, Canada's telecommunication carriers reacted to cable modem growth several years ago and have among the highest rates of take-up for DSL. Where the incumbent telecommunication carriers are outperformed by cable in other markets it would be expected that they will also have to significantly lift their performance if they wish to remain competitive.

Incumbent telecommunication carriers have had an ongoing stake in the cable television industry throughout the 1990s. Their peak participation was in 1998 when one in every five cable television customers across the OECD subscribed to a system owned by an incumbent telecommunication carrier. This was up from around 15% in 1993. If the overall percentage of telecommunication carrier ownership of cable networks seems small, it is worth noting that, in 1998, some 70% of all subscribers to cable networks outside of Canada, Japan, Korea and the United States were customers of incumbent telecommunication carriers. In the EU area, some 59% of the cable market was owned by incumbent telecommunication carriers in 1998.

Some of the carriers that entered the market between 1993 and 1998 were Ameritech, Bell South, Matav, Portugal Telecom, Siminn, Swisscom, Telstra, Telmex, Telecom Italia and Telecom New Zealand. Other incumbents, such as BT, France Telecom, Deutsche Telekom P&T Luxembourg, TDC, Telia, Telenor, Turk Telecom, had longer-standing ownership of cable networks systems.

Sometimes this had resulted from a national plan developed in their capacity as State-owned carriers, with monopolies over the provision of communications infrastructure. In other cases, the carriers were simply awarded franchises for certain regions, with independent cable companies operating in other areas. In some cases, such as Ameritech and Bell South, it was the result of deregulation, which allowed carriers to compete against existing cable networks.

Following its peak, in 1998, there has been a gradual decline in the incumbent telecommunication carrier share of the cable market. In some cases, this was the result of regulatory intervention, and in others a separate sale of the cable network at the time of privatisation of the incumbent. There were also instances of incumbents simply changing their commercial strategy and selling off or discontinuing to build cable networks.

An element in the latter phenomenon is that cable network ownership in home markets has not proved to be very financially rewarding, as a standalone business, for telecommunication carriers. As the telecommunication market evolves, with competition from multiple platforms, defensive plays in telephony may no longer justify a loss-making cable operation. One of the first incumbent telecommunication carriers to sell their cable network was in the Netherlands. When in 1997, KPN sold Casema to France Telecom. This sale was followed by BT, Eircom, Telmex, Swisscom selling their respective cable networks in the United Kingdom, Ireland, Mexico and Switzerland. In other cases, such as for Telecom New Zealand and Telecom Italia, fledgling cable networks were simply closed by those carriers.

In the United States, all the incumbent local exchanges carriers bar one that entered the cable market following the 1996 Telecommunications Act, had withdrawn by 2002. The exception was Bell South which maintained a very small cable network. Moreover France Telecom and Deutsche Telekom began selling cable assets.

The major change in the proportion of cable networks

owned by incumbents occurred in March 2003, when Deutsche Telekom sold its remaining cable networks. Following the sale Deutsche Telekom only had an equity position in one cable network in Germany. Deutsche Telekom's divestiture brought the total share of the cable market owned by telecommunication carriers down to a little over 5%. This number will fall further following the completion of the sale of TeliaSonera's cable network in Sweden. This is a requirement of the merger between of Telia and Sonera.

Even though the tide has turned on incumbent telecommunication carrier ownership of cable networks, they are still major players in just over one third of OECD countries. In April 2003, these countries were: Australia, Denmark, Finland, France, Hungary, Iceland, Luxembourg, Norway, Portugal, Sweden and Turkey. In Germany, the share of Deutsche Telekom is now very small, and in the United States, Bell South's market share is negligible.

In the one-third of countries with ongoing cable ownership by incumbent carriers, all are either the largest or second-largest players in the respective markets. In Australia, Denmark, Sweden and Portugal, the incumbents own the largest cable network. In Finland, Elisa and TeliaSonera both own cable networks, as does Matav in Hungary, Siminn in Iceland and Telenor in Norway. France Telecom, P&T Luxembourg and Turk Telekom own cable television networks as well as being the infrastructure provider for some other cable networks.

The impact of incumbent telecommunication carrier ownership of cable networks on the provision of cable telephony is very clear. For obvious reasons, cable networks owned by telecommunication carriers do not provide cable telephony. This service is, of course, already provided via the PSTN (Public Switched Telecommunication Network). By way of contrast, the same can not be said about the provision of Internet broadband access.

Unlike an existing service, such as telephony with an established platform, telecommunication carriers that own cable networks can choose how to provide broadband access over cable modems, DSL, or both. Their performance in doing so can be benchmarked against independently owned cable companies.

For policy makers, this assessment is necessary because, in those countries where telecommunication carriers own considerable shares of the cable sector, incumbents may own the only two available platforms that can readily provide broadband access. Regulated access, via tools such as unbundling and line sharing, can compensate to some extent but facilities competition is likely to lead to the best outcome. As one of the most important issues in communications is the development of broadband access, this analysis can help inform the question of why some countries are growing faster than others.

Performance of Cable Televisions Networks

To examine the performance of cable televisions networks, three indicators have been selected. These are cable modems, cable television and cable telephony. Data were collected for more than 50 cable television networks across the OECD, including those owned by incumbent telecommunication carriers and independently owned networks. Any networks owned by incumbents outside their "home country" were treated as independently owned networks. The indicator chosen to weight performance was the number of households passed by cable networks.

Cable Telephony

As noted it was not expected that there would be any cable telephony provided by incumbent telecommunication carriers and this, indeed, proved to be the case. It did, however, highlight those markets in which cable telephony is developing apace and those where independent cable companies are yet to introduce such a service. The companies with the highest take-up of cable telephony are Telewest and NTL in the United Kingdom. The other companies with a take-up rate higher than 20% of households passed are Optus in Australia, ONO Communications in Spain and Cabovisão in Portugal. Companies with between 10% and 20% are UPC (United Pan-Europe in Austria, RCN in the United States and Telenet in Belgium. While the leading performance of Telewest, NTL and Optus is commendable, it may also reflect the earlier date at which these companies were permitted to enter the telephony market. In the United Kingdom, cable companies entered the telephony market following the end of the telecommunications duopoly in 1992. In Australia, Optus entered the market as the second player during the country's telecommunications duopoly from 1992-97. Companies such as ONO in Spain and UPC (United Pan-Europe Communications) in Austria have only been permitted to offer telephony since 1998, with Cabovisão offering telephony from 2000 onwards.

Cable Television

Telecommunication carrier ownership of cable networks raises the question of how these networks perform, relative to independently owned cable networks, in the take-up of cable television. Unlike cable telephony or even cable modems, there is nothing intrinsic to hold back a telecommunication carrier's performance in cable television service. On the other hand, as cable television is not a core business of telecommunication carriers, it is unlikely to be a priority in a number of respects. In addition, some carriers may enter or maintain their position in the cable television market to defend their telecommunications market rather than run cable networks with maximum efficiency.

As might be expected, independently owned cable television networks have a higher take-up rate than those owned by incumbent telecommunication carriers. However the difference is not large. Independent networks, on average, have a take-up rate of 56% whereas those owned by telecommunication carriers have a 50% take-up rate..

The independent companies with the leading take-up of cable television are in the Netherlands, Belgium and Switzerland. In respect to cable companies, in which telecommunication carriers are involved, the two best performers are in Germany. Both these companies were among the first in which Deutsche Telekom sold majority interests. A number of networks have low take-up rates for cable television. Interestingly, some of the independent companies with the best take-up rates for cable telephony have a low take-up rate for cable television. The take-up rate for Optus is only 11% of households passed. In Spain, ONO has only managed to sign up 16.9% of households passed. In New Zealand, TelstraClear has a relatively low take-up rate as do both the cable companies in the United Kingdom.

In respect to cable networks owned by telecommunication carriers, a number have low take-up rates. In Iceland, only 15.7% of households take Siminn's cable television service. This may be because all available Icelandic channels are freely available and only foreign channels are subscription based. In Australia, Telstra also has a very low take-up on its cable television network, with just 19.2% of households passed subscribing to the service. Telstra attributes this, in part, to access and programme regulation.

On the supply side, Telstra says that regulated third-party access to pay television channels has discouraged ongoing investment in cable networks. On the demand side, Telstra says the strict regulation of premium sporting events on pay television, in favour of their availability on commercial free-to-air television, has dampened consumer take-up. In France, NC Numericable, which uses France Telecom's cable network to deliver service, also has a relatively low take-up rate.

One additional factor needs to be taken into account in the take-up rate for some companies. In a small number of cases, cable companies serve customers in the same area. This occurs in Australia, Portugal and a small number of areas in the United States. In the United States, RCN is a so-called, cable "over-builder" in some regions. In other words, RCN is a new entrant competing against an existing cable television provider. This explains why RCN has a lower take-up rate than most other cable companies in the United States.

In Australia, Telstra and Optus have an 80% overlap of their cable networks. Even then, the combined take-up rate for cable television is very low compared to other countries. In Portugal, cable networks also compete in the same area. There is a much higher take-up rate for cable television in Portugal than Australia. At the same time, Portugal Telecom and Cabovisão's take-up rates are relatively low in comparison with many companies. In both Australia and Portugal, competition between cable telephony and the PSTN has developed apace but the overall take-up of cable television is lower.

To the extent that the incumbent telecommunication carrier is in the cable market in these two countries, as a defensive play in respect to telecommunications, this may be a factor in why there is a lower take-up of cable television. This can be the result, for example, if the incumbent carrier was in the cable market primarily to defend their telecommunications revenue rather than to develop cable television. In this situation, the objective may be to slow growth of the competitor in adjacent markets rather than to necessarily maximise the incumbent telecommunication carrier's delivery of cable television. On the other hand, as Telstra notes, the attractiveness of cable television to consumers can be influenced by regulation that requires some of the most popular content to be shown on free-to-air television.

Cable Modems

Cable companies in Canada have attained the leading take-up of cable modems, in terms of homes passed. Shaw Communications provides cable modem service to just over one in every four households passed by their network. Rogers Communications has connected one in every five homes. At the end of 2002, these two companies were the only cable operators in the OECD to have a take up rate greater than 20% of all households passed.

The only broadband access provider with a higher take-up rate is Korea Telecom. At the end of 2002, KT had connected the equivalent of one in every three Korean households using DSL. Hanaro Telecom, using a combination of cable modems and DSL has a performance similar to the Canadian cable companies in terms of take-up.

The cable companies with the next best performance are UPC in Austria as well as GCI and Cablevision in the United States. Telenet and UPC in Belgium also have relatively high take-up rates. The striking feature of all the cable companies with leading performance is that they are in markets where there is strong competition between cable and DSL. They are also all independently owned cable companies. The best performing cable network that is owned by a telecommunication carrier is Portugal Telecom. However that company's performance presents a striking contrast to independently owned networks. Just over one in 20 households passed by Portugal Telecom's network takes cable modem service. Portugal Telecom's performance is followed by TeliaSonera in Finland and France Telecom. However, at this rate the take-up is very low, with TDC, Telenor and Telstra recording just one cable modem subscriber for every 33 households passed.

The ownership of cable television networks by incumbent telecommunication carriers has had quantifiable impacts on the development of broadband access. The average take-up rate for cable modems on networks owned by telecommunication carriers is just 2.6%. By way of contrast, the average for independently owned cable networks is 10.7%. In other words, if their home is passed by an independently owned cable company, users are four times more likely to take cable modem service.

The take-up rate for cable modem service on cable networks operated by telecommunication carriers is very poor relative to independently owned networks. In some cases this is because telecommunication carriers prefer to market DSL but this is not always the case. Telecom Portugal, for example, has many more cable modem subscribers than DSL subscribers. Telstra has around the same number of cable modem and DSL subscribers. This is not, however, the point. Where incumbent carriers have a preference for DSL, this translates into the cable network being severely under-utilised as a platform for providing broadband Internet access.

Moreover in the absence of a competitive platform or mechanisms that are working to efficiently open up local networks (*e.g.* unbundling, line sharing), the available evidence shows that incumbents develop DSL at a slower pace in those areas. This is due to a lack of competition from independently owned cable networks.

Where independently owned infrastructure or unbundling is at work, incumbents owning cable networks will work harder in those regions. Driven by unbundling and competition in some regions from independent infrastructure, TDC and TeliaSonera both had take-up rates of around one in ten homes for DSL at the end of 2002. However, if their cable companies were independently owned, all the evidence suggests they would also have a take-up rate of at least that magnitude. In Denmark, where TeliaSonera is not the incumbent, it had 12.8% take-up rate in 2002. In Sweden, at the same time, UPC had a take-up rate of 14.6%.

If UPC Sweden's take-up rate was applied to an independently owned ComHem an additional 323 000 modem users would have been in place. If TeliaSonera's Danish take-up rate was applied to TDC an additional 120 000 subscribers would have had cable modem service. The overall gains would, of course, have been higher because TeliaSonera and TDC would have had to compete more vigorously with DSL in those areas where they own both available platforms.

Accordingly, the point is not that incumbents may prefer one platform to another but rather that a readily available platform is severely under-utilised. Finally, the evidence suggests that any proposal to structurally separate cable networks along the lines that have been suggested for telecommunication networks, would not be advantageous. It is noticeable that where there is a separation of network facilities or a split between infrastructure and services the take-up of cable modem service is very low.

4

Media in Modern Democracy

The mass media constitute the backbone of democracy. The media are supplying the political information that voters base their decisions on. They identify problems in our society and serve as a medium for deliberation. They are also the watchdogs that we rely on for uncovering errors and wrongdoings by those who have power. It is therefore reasonable to require that the media perform to certain standards with respect to these functions, and our democratic society rests on the assumption that they do.

The following are the most important democratic functions that we can expect the media to serve.

— surveillance of sociopolitical developments,

— identifying the most relevant issues,

— providing a platform for debate across a diverse range of views,

— holding officials to account for the way they exercise power,

— provide incentives for citizens to learn, choose,

— become involved in the political process, and

— resist efforts of forces outside the media to subvert their independence.

Media critics claim that commercial mass media have become an antidemocratic force supporting the status quo. The news are more entertaining than informing, supplying mostly gossip, scandals, sex, and violence. Political news are more about personalities than about their ideologies. In the absence of serious debate, voters are left with paid political propaganda containing only meaningless slogans making them disinterested and cynical about politics. It is also claimed that the watchdogs are barking of the wrong things. The media hunt for scandals in the private lives of politicians and their families, but ignore much more serious consequences of their policies. They go after wounded politicians like sharks in a feeding frenzy.

All too often, the media make us afraid of the wrong things. Minor dangers are hysterically blown out of proportions, while much more serious dangers in our society go largely unnoticed. The exaggerated fears often lead to unnecessary measures and legislation and "gonzo justice" . Critics also complain that the media fail to report wrongdoings in the industry. For example, many media have suppressed information about the health hazards of smoking due to pressure from advertisers.

Freedom of Mass Media

The right to the freedom of speech/expression, as well as the freedom of the press, as a corollary of this right, represents fundamental values of the modern pluralist democracy. Without them, many of the progresses achieved in the contemporary world couldn't be imagined. That is why all these rights must be defended. However, these rights that were hard to acquire in the difficult process of democracy's birth, are nowadays abusively exercised in subtle forms by one of their major beneficiary which should have been one of their main defenders: the mass-media.

Social democracy states that the freedom of the press, as well as the freedom of expression, are essential for the defense and development of democracy. The experience of the last decade in Central Europe, for example, shows that mass media served decisively in the construction of the civil society and in censuring the authoritarian trends of some politicians or parties. Also, it corrected and continues to correct, the excesses, negligences and management errors in the countries with a consolidated democracy. Without the freedom of expression, and thus without the freedom of mass media, a democracy cannot be conceived. A free press sometimes makes difficult a democratic government's life or the life of public personalities; it always makes a dictatorship impossible.

In the context of these statements it must though be noticed that democracy is passing, at present, through a crisis of growth and of adaptation to the new contemporary world realities. The causes of this crisis are:

i. the inadequacy of the mechanisms of the democracy developed in the national environment to the conditions of globalizations;

ii. the occurrence, in the context of emergent globalization, of social communities who, fearing they will not be able to adapt to the new conditions, are sensitive to the populist and national-populist message;

iii. the weakening of the credibility and even of the efficiency of democracy's classic mechanisms because of the lack of transparency, electoralization and commercialization of the political action.

As for the third cause, it must be underlined that the invasion of the democratic exercise by the methods of the commercial marketing and the development of "show state" led to the wider separation of society from the political field and of the power from the truth. This fact is expressed by the low turn out at the elections, the civic non-involvement and the cynical views of the social actors. In respect of all these three causes, mass media has an immense responsibility and an essential role to play.

Mass media has some responsibilities as far as the crisis of the democracy is concerned. This is related at least to the following aspects:

— Mass media makes it possible the appearance and the development of the "political show". Electoralism means the exaltation of the elections' importance, not as a method for the consultation of the electorate in order to identify its aspirations and expectations, but only as a method of seizing the power. The power without a mandate regarding the application of a clear program is, though, a power that cannot be exercised. On medium and long term, such a power alienates the electorate; as it creates the feeling the voters have no control over politicians.

— Mass media might create as well, false personalities and destroy real personalities. It might impose questionable political groups and hide compromising truths, inventing, at the same time, artificial crises.

— Mass media sometimes could determine the spending of important amounts of money in campaign that might confuse the ordinary people and, thus, might actually encourage corruption.

— Mass media, in a number of cases, distorts reality and induces pessimism, skepticism, distrust and an inclination towards isolation and violence in society through its mainly conflictual approaches and its search for the sensation.

It is always very disturbing when mass media tries to determine the issues on the public agenda. Often artificially and without any relation with the citizens' real agenda and the priorities recommended by the social reality mass media attempts to establish political priorities. This fact can be explained, among others, by the secret links between mass media and the great national or international corporations. In such cases, although introducing itself as representing a public interest, mass media actually represents the private interests. This situation can lead to manipulations of the public opinion in the direction desired by the private financial sponsors, who are looking for some market advantages or economic gains. Therefore, the social-democracy must state that the freedom of the press is not reduced to its independence in relation to the public power, but it must also include its independence in relation to the private interests. On the other hand, the emergence of media monopolies creates the premises of reducing the number of options available to the citizen and the possibility of his subtle manipulation. The quality of information decreases and the danger of disorienting the citizen increases, as the very laws of competition on the free market are not protecting the press consumer any longer. This means, at the same time, the decrease in the quality of democracy.

All these negative phenomena - ever more serious as globalization advances and the press conveys events happening at long distance, events that the receiver cannot check directly – should lead to the recognition, besides the right to free information, to the freedom of expression and the freedom of the press, of a citizen's right to accurate information. In light of such a right, social democrats should support the following:

— The recognition of the fact that the activity of the press is an activity of public interest and, therefore, it must be carried out in accordance with some professional norms, at the level of some deontological standards and under a specific public control. Political institutions that are parts of the governmental or parliamentary systems, though, may not exercise such a control. Only the judicial courts and the civil society may do it.

— The recognition of an individual right of recourse to a competent court for each person having a legitimate interest in a correct information.

— The adoption of special regulations regarding the fight aginst the conflict of interests in the field of mass media. According to these regulations, the property or co-property, as well as the participation in the administration of some media instruments by those who are active in the political life or by those who are owners or majoritary shareholders in commercial societies of another profile, among others, should be banished.

— The adoption of special anti-trust laws for the media institutions. To this purpose, the media trusts holding a television or radio station with a national audience would be forbidden to own national papers, or vice versa. Also, any cartelization or commercial or editorial policy ententes agreed by several media institutions should be forbidden. The conventions according to which a press institution will not criticize the position of another or will not denounce the information errors of another will be considered fully void.

— The adoption of regulations regarding the obligation of a previous (ex ante) checking of the news by consulting before the news are published, all those interested, as well as the obligation of granting the right to reply for all those who by doing that can preserve their good name or can defend other legitimate interests. Through the same regulations the right privacy for public personalities and for other citizens, as well as the means of defending this specific right, would be defined. The balance between the freedom of access to information, the right to a free expression of opinions and the benefit of doubt should be established through special norms, as well.

— The organization of professional institutions of journalists and the adoption of Deontological Codes of the mass media. The breach of the duties established by such codes could be sanctioned by special "press tribunals" formed by the journalists themselves, which, upon the inquiry of the applications laid by concerned persons, could apply moral, professional or pecuniary sanctions, according to each case.

— The establishment at the international level and by the international fora and institutions, of international professional and deontological standards in this field, such as to avoid the subjectivity always emerging from the internal political competition.

By endorsing such measures, at the same time with measures aiming at defending the freedom of the press, the mass media will contribute to the essential process of "democratizing democracy", a process that is necessary in the context of globalization and of the crisis that the traditional democratic mechanisms are facing.

Meida Economics

Mass media get most or all of their income from advertisements and sponsoring. Therefore they will seek to optimally satisfy the interests of their advertisers, which are not necessarily coincident with the interests of the readers, listeners and viewers. The predominant view among economists is that free competition generally benefits society because it provides the most differentiated supply of commodities to the optimal price. This line of reasoning dominates European as well as American media policy. It is well known, however, that free competition does not always consider all interests.

The term market failure describes the situation where the free market forces do not automatically lead to maximal welfare. For example, this may be the case when consumers are unable to evaluate the quality of a commodity. In this case the market forces will lead to a sub-optimal quality; and a political intervention such as required informative labelling or minimum standards of quality might be justified. Another example of market failure is when third party interests are affected, as in the case of pollution or depletion of natural resources. In the case of media financed by advertisements exclusively, the interests served are those of the advertisers. The interests of the media consumers are satisfied only insofar as these are coincident with the interests of the advertisers. There is no guarantee that public interests are served well. This is the reason why many countries have public radio- and TV stations with public service obligations.

A policy, which is often used for the express purpose of making sure that all interests are served, is liberalizing the media market and relying on the free market forces. Many theorists ignore, however, that the media not only satisfy consumer preferences, but also form them. Many economists assume that competition increases diversity. Numerous policy discussions recommend increased competition as the best way to assure diversity which, it is assumed, will make sure that all interests are served well. However, this strategy has failed time and again because the underlying assumptions are wrong.

It has been known for many years that there is a strong tendency towards wasteful duplication of the most popular program forms under free competition. There is considerable disagreement over whether competition increases or decreases the diversity of media products. While moderate competition may increase diversity, it has been found theoretically as well as empirically that excessive competition may lead to decreased diversity. Assume, for example, that a country has two competing commercial TV-stations with each one channel. In this case they will both try to maximize their market share by sending the same kind of programs that appeal to the broadest possible audience. But if, on the other hand, both channels are owned by the same TV-station, then the owner will seek to minimize competition between the two channels by sending different types of programs on the two channels.

Most studies of the effect of market structure on the quality of mass media products use diversity as the only measure of satisfaction of consumer needs. Diversity is the most objective criterion and the one that is most easily measured. Some authors explicitly state their unwillingness to use more subjective quality measures, but at least one scientist has demonstrated that it can be done.

Diversity may indeed be a poor measure of quality. If we assume that there is a positive relationship between production costs and the quality of a media product, and if we further assume that the total revenue from a particular niche of the media market is limited, then we can conclude that the more competitors there are to share the niche, the less income will each competitor have to spend on improving quality. There may in fact be a negative relationship between diversity and quality. It has been criticized that the diversity that is measured is a diversity of form, not of contents, and even less does it represent a diversity of opinions or ideologies, nor a satisfaction of consumer interests.

A diversity of program formats is hardly related to fairness, relevance, thorough investigation, or other requirements that we expect a democratic press to meet. The available studies of diversity therefore fail to capture the central problems related to the democratic role of the media. It is necessary that media economists introduce other quality measures in studies of the relationship between market structure and the quality of mass media products. Lacking better criteria, we may use production costs as a reasonable measure of quality.

Many of the mathematical models are based on the assumption that a TV program or other media product satisfying a specific demand is produced at fixed costs. The product is either produced or not produced, depending on whether it is profitable. This simplification fails to cover the easily observable fact that a media product satisfying a specific demand may be produced in varying degrees of quality at varying costs. If many competitors share the same product niche then each competitor will have less income to cover production costs and will therefore be forced to make a product of lower quality. With fewer competitors it may be possible, and perhaps also profitable, to make a product of higher quality. For example, if many competitors share the market for political news, then each competitor will have few resources for investigative journalism and will only be able to uncritically relay the messages from politicians and news agencies. Several studies have found a negative correlation between competition and news quality.You may expect that at least free competition leads at to an optimal satisfaction of the interests of the advertisers, but this is not always the case.

Theoretical calculations show that free competition may favor products with high variable costs rather than products with high fixed costs, because as the number of suppliers gets higher, each supplier has less income for covering the fixed costs. When applied to mass media, this means that more competition may lead to lower quality if we assume that there is a positive correspondence between production costs and quality. Several observations confirm this. If we assume that media products of higher quality can attract a larger audience, then we must conclude that excessive competition benefits neither consumers nor advertisers.

Denmark is regarded as a good test case because it had a state monopoly TV station until 1988 when one, and later more, commercial TV stations were introduced. The introduction of competing TV stations were motivated by the desire to improve the quality and diversity of the program supply and to make sure that minority interests were satisfied.

A government commission recommended competition as the means to obtain these goals, in spite of the fact that they were aware of experiences from England and Sweden showing that competition might reduce program quality. The commission was not aware of any theory that could explain this effect. A recent investigation has shown that the competition has not improved the quality of news productionas predicted by Sepstrup. In Sweden, where the market situation is similar, it has been observed that TV news have become more dramatic, sensationalist, and less informative, as the competition has increased.

Media Market Developments

The development of the mass media during the last decades is characterized by the following main tendencies:

— *Convergence*: Different media, like newspapers, radio, television, telephone and internet are increasingly being fused together, technologically as well as economically.

— *Concentration*: Media companies are being merged together and controlled by fewer owners. This concentration is horizontal (several media under the same owner) as well as vertical (several links in the "food chain" under the same company group). Different media bring news from the same sources.

— *Globalization*: The media are owned by multinational companies broadcasting across borders.

— *Commercialization*: Advertisements are sneaked into entertainment as well as news stories. The distinctions between advertisements, news and entertainment are increasingly blurred. Audience groups with less spending money are not considered.

— *Commercial influence*: Advertisers and owners have influence on editorial decisions.

— *Trivialization*: More sex and violence. More prying into the private lives of celebrities. The media avoid controversial issues and serious debates. Debates are reduced to an entertaining clash between personalities, resembling a boxing match, where the issue of controversy has only secondary importance.

Several media scholars agree that the main cause of these tendencies is the liberalization of the media market.

Popularization

The simulation of proximity is an important element in popularization. A political decision can be difficult to explain in abstract terms. It helps when the medium shows an ordinary person telling what the consequences of the decision is for him or her. The audience feel that a story is more convincing when they see an example they can identify with. But in fact it is less credible, because the example may not be representative.

A magazine can show a person who felt better after taking a certain brand of alternative medicine, and fail to show the 99% who felt worse after taking the same medicine. Advertising has a profound influence on the choice of programs. TV advertisers prefer to have their commercials shown in association with soft entertainment. Ideal from the advertisers' point of view are shows such as competitions where you can win sponsored merchandise, or soap operas that portray a privileged lifestyle where luxurious goods give status. This does not provide good conditions for the political debate.

It is difficult to find sponsors for serious political debates because these do not make the viewers relax and because some of the viewers will disagree with the points of view presented. Furthermore, the commercial media are not very inclined to cover controversial issues in a balanced way. People prefer to hear points of view that they agree with. It is therefore adverse to the media's economy to view a controversy from both sides and present alternative points of view.

The media are prone to choose side in a controversy, and if later evidence should favor the opposite side, they are likely to keep silent about the matter rather than loosing face. Disclaimers are not profitable. This is a self-amplifying process. The more the media create consensus about a particular issue through biased coverage, the fewer proponents of the opposite view will there be to balance the issue, and the more difficulties will these proponents have in gaining access to the media. Nowhere is this bias problem worse than in crime reporting. The media often take a stance on the question of guilt before a verdict has been made. The police and the prosecutor are often very willing to express themselves because it gives them a PR gain and an opportunity to ask the public for help in solving crimes, while the suspect has few, if any, possibilities and resources for replying. It is very unlikely that judges can resist being influenced by this when a media frenzy has created a public outcry against a suspect.

The legal possibilities of forcing the media to publish disclaimers or to give a voice to alternative points of view are quite illusory, and the means of sanctions are far from effective. The printed media cannot compete with the ability of the electronic media to keep their audience spellbound by strong sense impressions.

The newspapers have their strength in the possibilities for in-dept analysis of social and other topics. However, this possibility is not fully exploited because the journalistic resources are limited by economic competition, and because this parameter of competition only gives access to a limited niche of the reader market. Many papers and magazines therefore compete on news about celebrities and topics that appeal to the emotions. Everything that is dangerous, deviant or wrong has a prominent place, especially in those papers that are mainly sold from newsstands. They want to have a new scandal on the front page every day in order to tempt people to buy the paper. We may expect to see similar approaches when electronic pay-per-view media become common.

Radio- and TV-channels based on advertising use fewer horror effects, because this would conflict with the principle of bringing the viewers into a buying-mood. This does not improve the journalistic and artistic quality, however. Many media workers are frustrated that their creativity is curbed by the economic structures, and the situation is hardly better for advertisement-free commercial media, such as home video and pay-TV.

Selection Criteria

Traditionally, media scholars have described the selection of news with concepts like gatekeeping and newsworthiness. These concepts are based on a scenario where an editor or journalist sorts incoming news according to news value and political criteria. Social problems involving fear and danger are very attractive to the media and such topics often make up a significant part of the stories. The excessive focus on fear and danger has important political implications. The dissemination of news may occasionally be so selective and biased that you may accuse the media of manipulation and propaganda, for example in connection with war. But in general we do not have to impute dishonest motives on producers in order to explain media distortion. Most cases of selection in the news media can be explained by structural factors, such as the organization of news agencies, financing, dependence on sources, and ratings competition.

The news coverage is determined by such factors as the journalist's knowledge, predefined news formats, deadlines, the authority of sources, and the possibility of obtaining good pictures. The media may not publish a story if it does not fit into an existing format or if it does not relate to an existing theme. The media are self-referential to such a degree that the newsworthiness of a story may be a self-fulfilling prophecy. A topic is interesting because all the media tell about it. Violent crimes and sex crimes are areas where the news reporting is highly selective. The media prefer emotional stories, weeping victims, and stories that fit into the political agenda and confirm the image of the criminal as a monster. The use of expert sources has been found to be extraordinarily selective.

The media play a key role in the public debate on risks and dangers, but their coverage is highly selective. At times the media exaggerate minor risks where reassurance would be more sensible. In other cases they ignore serious risks, e.g. when new technologies are uncritically described as progress. It is an essential problem when informing about risks and dangers that the concept is abstract and invisible until it manifests itself in a specific accident or disaster. The media do not like to report on hypothetical risks. They need a real event that the theoretical discussion can be related to and real people to give the story a human-interest dimension.

Risk analysts have been criticized for ignoring these problems and not focusing enough on the mass media. The media may be attracted to risks, but not unconditionally so. They are not good at maintaining attention to a theoretical risk when there are no actual events to make the topic newsworthy. There is an unusually fierce competition between sources when it comes to informing about risks, dangers and other social problems. Various interest groups, politicians and experts seek to promote each their agenda on which dangers to fear. The media inevitably play a key role in this conflict because their choice of sources influences the definition of risks. The politicians have to take a stance to whatever problem the media place high on the agenda. The media's decision on who is allowed to define a problem, or whether the problem is mentioned at all, is not controlled in a democratic way.

Cultural selection theory is a theory that explains social change based on selection events. Humans may make conscious decisions based on intelligent planning as well as unconscious or irrational decisions. All decisions count as selection events. Selection events can also be caused by external influences, the environment, or be necessitated by the logic of the social structure.

The systematic study of selection mechanisms shows that the combined effect of many small selection events can bring about macroscopic changes in the social structure. These social changes are often planned and beneficial, but they may as well be unplanned, unexpected and undesired. An important advantage of cultural selection theory over other models of social change is that it better explains undesired developments.

When applying this theory to the mass media, we already

know that news and stories are selected by the media, and the selection criteria have already been discussed. But there is also a selection going on at a higher level, namely the economic competition between mass media.

The relentless economic competition forces the media to concentrate on those topics that immediately catch our attention and make us buy today's newspaper or stay tuned on the TV channel through the commercial breaks. Serious quality media that do not mesmerize their audience with psychological means get fewer customers and thus less revenue from advertisements. The reduced income forces them to cut down the journalist staff whereby the quality is reduced and more readers or viewers fall away. This vicious circle continues until the medium goes bankrupt or changes its policy.

The economic selection that results from competition between news media is taking place at a higher level than the selection decisions of journalists and other gatekeepers. The economic selection may therefore be able to override the selection at the lower level by forcing those media organizations out of business that do not let economic considerations determine their selection and shaping of stories. This means that the media can and do develop in directions that no journalist or editor wishes. Many journalists are frustrated by the increasing tabloidization of their media and try to improve the standards, but to no avail.

We now know that those media that survive on the conditions of a free market economy are the ones that are best at catching people's attention. But what are the criteria for a story that catches our attention? The study of what catches our attention most, reveals that our primitive instincts actually play an important role. Some of the most important survival factors for primeval man were food, danger, sex, and children. It is deeply ingrained in every human being that these topics catch our attention wherever we meet them, according to Richard

Brodie. For example, it has always been of vital importance to collect knowledge about everything that is dangerous. Therefore, we listen attentively when the TV tells about disasters, and we always buy the newspaper when the front page tells about dangerous criminals. Such attention-catching topics are metaphorically called buttons.

A story that sells well is said to push our most sensitive buttons. There are other buttons as well, but the four mentioned above are the most important ones. A branch of cultural selection theory called memetics studies how certain ideas and stories are propagated preferentially in a culture. Scholars of memetics have found that those stories that push the right buttons are much more contagious than other stories.

This discovery is very much in agreement with the findings of media scholars of what the preferred topics in trivialized media are. Brodie's list of sensitive buttons also has marked similarities with Habermas' list of attention-catching subjects and some similarities with Luhmann's observations as well.

Brodie's theory is based on evolutionary psychology- a discipline that was unknown when Habermas wrote down his observations.These buttons are found everywhere in the media and entertainment industry. A plethora of politicians, interest groups, charity organizations, religious groups, PR agents and advertisers are incessantly competing for our attention. Those who can hold their own in this fierce competition are the ones who can push the right buttons - which is not necessarily the ones who have the most important messages to tell.

The psychological appeal in the media lies not only in the choice of topics but also in the way they are framed. A message is more appealing when it is focused on a real person that people can identify with.

Therefore, the media prefer to give a story a personal angle rather than discussing abstract principles. Thus, political debates are often presented as personal conflicts between politicians rather than as discussions about ideologies. The personality, private life, and media appeal of a politician thus becomes more important than his ideological stance.

Media Influence

There are many different theories about how mass media influence people's attitudes, worldview, and behavior. Many studies have found that the media have little power to change people's opinions, but more power to reinforce existing views. This leads to the important question: How are the views formed in the first place? One may hypothesize that the media have a strong effect the first time a new issue is discussed. In fact, several studies have found that media effects are stronger for issues that people are unfamiliar with. Communication studies have traditionally been divided between the study of mass media and the study of interpersonal communication. Recently, it has been argued that this is a false dichotomy because the mass media may inspire interpersonal communication. Rogers attributes the findings of many studies that mass media effects are small to the fact that they do not include the secondary effect of interpersonal communication.

In fact, the two-step flow model of communication has been known for many years:

> The mass media influence some people who, in turn, influence other people. A few recent studies have found very strong media effects in cases where the media have prompted people to discuss an issue with their families and friends.
>
> The influence of the media is not unidirectional. Among the people influenced by the media are the elites and opinion leaders whose opinions appear in the mass media.

> This circular flow of communication may obviously amplify certain opinions. Another selfamplifying process is the "spiral of silence". Noelle-Neumann discovered that people might be reluctant to voice unpopular opinions for fear of social isolation. This effect may cause the amplification of mainstream opinions or opinions that are perceived as growing in popularity, while minority opinions are suppressed. Such a mechanism may explain fashions and fads. Several studies have measured the "spiral of silence" effect by asking people whether they would voice their opinion in a hypothetical situation. These studies have found a quite weak, though significant, effect. One field study, which placed unsuspecting people in a situation where they were actually asked to present their opinion, found a stronger effect. Members of a minority were less willing to express their opinion towards members of a majority than vice versa.

These secondary effects, some stronger than others, all point in the same direction:

> The effect of the mass media is stronger when secondary effects are taken into account than when the direct effect of media messages on each individual are measured.

While historical as well as contemporary observations are full of examples attesting to the power of the mass media to influence people, early experimental studies have failed to confirm the assumption that mass media have a strong power to change people's attitudes. This discrepancy between experiments and real world observations was solved with the introduction of theories of cognitive processing, such as agenda setting, framing, and priming.

Cognitive Processing

The newsmedia contain huge amounts of information, much more than any person can possibly handle. It is therefore theorized that humans are economizing the processing of the information they receive from newsmedia as well as from other sources. The first step in the handling of information is selection. People chose which newsmedia to read, watch, and listen to, according to their needs and preferences. They are screening the media for interesting information, ignoring topics that appear to be irrelevant to them, redundant, boring, or too complicated to comprehend. People routinely reject stories that appear too remote or too complicated simply to save time and energy. Stories that catch people's attention are those that are relevant to their personal interests, but also general human-interest stories such as reports about crimes and accidents, health, sports, entertainment, and celebrities. The producers of news have learned to snare people's attention by giving most stories a personal touch.

Once a story has been selected for attention, the cognitive processing of the story is further economized by schematic thinking. Humans use what has been called knowledge structures or schemata as mental templates that people and events are fitted into. This process facilitates the integration of new information into existing knowledge. Since news sources usually present the news in isolated snippets without sufficient background, the schemata allow the receivers to embed the news in a meaningful context. This process also facilitates discarding redundant information that already exists in the schema as well as information that conflicts with previous knowledge that still appears to be sound. People often misunderstand stories, either because they do not have an appropriate schema for interpreting the story, or because they apply the schema that comes first to mind rather than the schema that is most appropriate. Well-informed people have a rich collection of schemata that makes it easier to process new information. Thus, the information-rich become still richer.

Agenda-setting

The effect of agenda-setting is epitomized in the famous quote by Bernard Cohen, saying that the press "may not be successful much of the time in telling people what to think, but it is stunningly successful in telling its readers what to think about" . People need to orient themselves in a complex world full of complex issues. In the absence of other cues, people tend to judge the importance of issues from their salience in the media and to focus their attention on those presumably most important issues. There is plenty of evidence that the media have a strong influence on people's perception of which issues are important and which problems they want their government to do something about.

The agenda-setting influence of the news media increases when the need for orientation among the audience is high. The agenda-setting effect is lower for obtrusive issues that people can observe directly, as well as for other issues that the audience is well informed about. The media have little power to set the agenda when people have sufficient political knowledge to counterargue the claims made by the media. Furthermore, the agenda-setting effect is stronger for concrete issues that are easy to visualize than for abstract issues.

While the powerful effect of agenda-setting is generally accepted among media scholars, there is some uncertainty about who sets the agenda. Some studies show that politicians have a strong influence on the agenda of mass media, at least in areas such as economic policy. But, as discussed in the preceding paragraphs, the media may themselves put attention-catching issues on the agenda for economic reasons, especially sensationalistic issues such as danger, crime, sex, and celebrity scandals. Access to the public agenda is a limited and precious resourcethat special interest groups often compete for, as discussed below.

Priming

Priming refers to the fact that one piece of media information can influence how we interpret subsequent pieces of information by making us tune in to certain areas of thought. Thus, the news media can influence the criteria by which political candidates are judged by calling attention to some issues and ignoring others before the speech of the candidate. For example, the support for president Bush dropped significantly in 1992 because an intense media focus on economic recession made voters shift from evaluating the president in terms of his handling of the Gulf war to evaluating his handling of national economy. The priming effect is often explained in terms of schematic thinking. When evaluating new information or making a decision, people tend to apply the information and schemata that are most readily accessible or available in memory at that moment, rather than conduct a complete and comprehensive search and examination of information. A schema may be readily accessible to the individual either because it has recently been activated and remains in shortterm memory, or because it is linked in memory to other constructs which have been activated.

Framing

Framing refers to the frame of reference within which an issue is described. For example, a news broadcast about the development of new nuclear weapons can variously be framed as a story about technological progress, about military budgets, about military strategy, about balance of power between nations, about arms race versus disarmament, or about radiation hazards. The way the story is framed can have a strong influence on people's attitudes towards the issue. It is often assumed that framing is a kind of second-level agenda setting in the sense that it makes certain aspects of an issue more salient in such a way as to promote a particular problem definition.

However, it has been argued that framing influences how audiences think about issues, not by making aspects of the issue more salient, but by determining which schemata are activated in the interpretation of the incoming information. While the former definition of framing implies that the effect of framing is likely to be intentional, the latter model implies that framing is based on subtle nuances in wording and syntax so that the effect of framing is most likely unintentional.

Since every story must have a frame, whether the journalist pays attention to framing or not, we cannot assume that the effects of framing are always intentional. Several theorists make a distinction between frames in the media and frames in the minds of the audience. A media frame is "a central organizing idea or story line that provides meaning to an unfolding strip of events..." Audience frames are defined as "mentally stored clusters of ideas that guide individuals' processing of information" . These definitions should be preferred because they have a better theoretical foundation and because they make no assumption about whether a particular media frame is intended to promote a particular audience frame. A review of the studies on framing finds that the concept is often vaguely defined and there is more research to do. On the other hand, the review leaves no doubt that framing in some cases can have a profound effect on the attitudes, worldview, and behavior of the audience.

The commercialization and trivialization of news media has a strong influence on how issues are framed in the commercial news media. Framing political news around the strategies of politicians rather than issues makes the audience perceive the motives of politicians as egoistic, whereby a cynical view on politics may be fostered. Stories about social problems are often framed with a focus on people rather than principles, single events rather than themes, and easily understandable proximate causes rather than deeper and more complex causes. This choice of framing influences the attribution of responsibility for the problems, the causal attribution, and the remedies that will be chosen to ameliorate the problems in question.

The media will often find some person to blame for a problem, but without a deeper focus on the social structures that caused the problem, it is unlikely that an effective solution to the problem will be found and accepted. Entertainment abhors ambiguity. Once a particular interpretation has been applied to a conflict, it is unlikely that the media will reframe the issue. Without seeing an issue from more than one side, it is unlikely that the conflict or problem will be solved in a sensible way. The personalized framing of crime stories is likely to make the audience see the cause of the problem in moral defects of the perpetrator. The lack of focus on deeper causes such as poverty, discrimination, poor education, and blocked opportunities may keep the audience from suggesting more effective preventive remedies against crime.

The commercial need for personalization of stories also make the media focus on victims of crime. Grieving victims make good stories with a strong emotional appeal. The strongly emotional content of these stories is likely to evoke the primitive feelings of revenge in the audience and a call for stronger penalties, regardless of whether punitive measures can solve the problem. Crime reporting is just one example of this effect, and admittedly a controversial one. The pervasive media focus on people rather than principles, events rather than themes, and simple rather than deep causes, is adversely affecting the problem-solving capabilities of democratic societies on a broad variety of issues, ranging from poverty to international conflicts.

Cultivation Theory

Cultivation theory is a research tradition, which assumes that there are certain repetitive and pervasive patterns of images and ideologies dominating most genres of television shows and films. If people spend several hours a day, year after year, watching television, and if every show they watch is full of violence, then people may come to believe that the world is full of violence. This is the kind of hypotheses that cultivation studies are trying to prove. There can be no doubt that the television world is different from the real world. News and drama alike contain more crime and violence than the real world. The proportion of violent crimes to nonviolent crimes is much higher in TV than in the real world. The characters portrayed in TV drama are not representative of the population at large. There are more men than women and an over-representation of people in prestigious professions. Numerous studies have found that heavy TV-viewers tend to over-estimate the amount of violence in society, the risk of falling victim to a violent crime, the fraction of the population engaged in law enforcement, the fraction of the population with prestigious professions, the fraction of the population that have marital discords and extramarital affairs, etc. The observed effects are relatively weak, but consistent and statistically significant.

The effects of receiving the high dose of crime and violence from television have been called the mean world syndrome. Heavy TV viewers may come to perceive the world as a gloomy and dangerous place. People become fearful of falling victim to violent crime and take drastic measures to protect themselves and their children - measures that are out of touch with the objective risk. The fearful people become authoritarian and easy victims of political manipulation. Many cultivation theorists assume that the pervasive patterns of TV images are shaped by commercial influence. Most cultivation studies are carried out in the USA where the commercial influence on television is strong. A few studies in countries where noncommercial television has a significant impact, find the "mean world" effect to be smaller than in the USA.

The hypothesis of commercial influence is further supported by a few international comparisons that find the cultivation effects to be stronger in countries where commercial television dominates than in countries with predominantly noncommercial television. The very broad-based focus has made cultivation studies vulnerable to criticism. The lumping together of all genres and all viewing patterns is likely to dilute the observed effect. This may be the reason why the observed correlations are weak. Evidently, some TV genres contain more violence than others, and different genres have different effects on people's worldview.

Critics of cultivation research point out that the correlations may be spurious, while adherents of the paradigm emphasize that no strong mediating variables have been found and that the results are quite stable over different research conditions. Most cultivation studies are based on surveys. A survey can prove correlation, but not causation. It is theoretically impossible to tell on the basis of a correlation between TV viewing habits and attitudes whether viewing habits influence attitudes, or attitudes influence viewing habits, or whether some unidentified extraneous variable influence both. In fact, one study, which observed an association between the viewing of crime drama and authoritarian aggression, found both directions of causality to be equally plausible.

The position of cultivation theorists towards the question of causality is sometimes quite inconsistent. Leading theorists state that causal models are impossible, or even irrelevant. Yet the same theorists discuss causal models all the time. In fact, the whole paradigm rests on the assumption that cultivation is a long-term cumulative effect, and this assumption makes no sense unless a direction of causality is assumed. An irrefutable proof for the direction of causality is only possible with experimental manipulation of TV viewing patterns. Unfortunately, most cultivation researchers discount such experimental studies because experiments focus on particularistic short-term effects, while the cultivation research project emphasizes the long-term combined effect of the viewing of all TV genres.

A few experimental studies have found significant effects of relatively short-term exposure on the attitudes of TV viewers, but most experimental studies are concerned with measuring behavior rather than attitudes. A strong indication of the direction of causality has recently been obtained, however, from an improved understanding of the cognitive mechanisms underlying the cultivation effect. These mechanisms, which have been confirmed experimentally, cannot easily be accounted for if the causality is spurious or reversed. When asked to estimate, for example, the incidence of violence in society, people tend to economize their mental processing effort and give a heuristic answer based on the ease with which instances of violence can be recalled. A number of testable predictions can be made from this model, and these predictions have been confirmed experimentally.

Experimental conditions that induce a more systematic information processing can make test persons discount TV as a reliable source of information and give more accurate answers. Likewise, it is known from cognitive psychology and endocrinology that concrete and emotional accounts make a stronger impression than abstract descriptions. In accordance with this theory, it has been found by experiments that people judge the incidence of particular phenomena by the number of examples in the media rather than by statistical accounts when both examples and statistics are presented in the media.

Medial Sociology

In the sociological theory of Jürgen Habermas, the mass media are controlled by political and economic forces, which have an interest in manipulating the audience. This compromises the legitimacy of the communicative power exercised by the mass media. The political manipulation is a kind of opinion making and PR, where the media not only transmit debates, but also create and shape them. The commercial manipulation uses the carefully designed and tested psychological methods of advertising.

The media explore themes and identification possibilities that appeal to the unconscious dispositions of the audience in order to attract attention. Habermas mentions the following themes as attracting common interest: romance, religion, money, children, health, and animals. The German political scientist Peter Klier criticizes Habermas' manipulation hypothesis because absolute objectivity does not exist. Klier thinks that the amount of information in modern society is so huge that media as well as citizens and politicians have to make a very strict selection. Members of the public can neither grasp the many topics, nor penetrate sufficiently deep into a particular topic to fulfill the role that they are supposed to, according to the norms of democracy.

Klier thinks that this selection is such a big problem that you do not need any manipulation hypothesis to conclude that democracy has a legitimacy problem. He stresses that people's reality image is more determined by the media-reality the more they are dependent on selective media and the less their chances are of getting corrective information from primary sources. Klier advocates this obvious observation as a counter thesis to the manipulation hypothesis. But this so-called counter thesis confirms the very fact that the media produce a skewed image of reality. We are only left with the question of whether this distortion deserves to be called manipulation.

Niklas Luhmann, in his social systems theory, sees communication as a fundamental process in any social system. The communication forms a triple selection process:

1. selection of information at the sender,
2. selective attention at the receiver,
3. the selecting effect of the received information.

The communication is very much controlled by the media in modern society. Luhmann describes the mass media as a self-referential and self-maintaining (autopoietic), almost autonomous system. Unfortunately, Luhmann does not go very far in his analysis of how this media system is integrated into the bigger social system. Luhmann finds that the most important selection criteria of the media are the following: surprising news, topicality, conflicts, quantitative data, local relevance, as well as scandals and norm violations in relation to individual actors and moral judgments. Luhmann is not clear in the question of whether the media distort reality, because he emphasizes that there is no objective measure to evaluate the media reports against. He tries to evade the problem by saying that the media are accused of manipulating, rather than just saying that they manipulate. We also have to accept that the media fit reality into certain frames of reference, because there is no other option.

However, this relativist line of thought does not deter Luhmann from giving specific examples of how the media influence society by their selectivity. He mentions the Golf war, AIDS, and immigrant crimes as examples. He even recognizes that the media may provide falsehoods if the need for news and sensations overweigh the risk that the deception be revealed. Unfortunately, Luhmann only mentions the role of the mass media superficially in his book on risk sociology. Here the selectivity of the media is only mentioned in a footnote, and he is ambivalent to claims of distortions, although he recognizes exaggerations as well as understatements.

Risk Sociology

Because of the prominence of the topics of risk and danger in the mass media, and because of the important political implications of the intense focus and possible exaggeration of certain dangers, we may find it worthwhile to look more into these areas of study. If we want to study the possibly exaggerated fear of certain dangers and risks generated by the media, it seems obvious to turn to the risk sociology that is based on Ulrich Beck's book Risk Society and Mary Douglas' Purity and Danger . Unfortunately, Beck does not pay much interest to exaggerations of risks. His project is, on the contrary, to investigate understatements of risks. Admittedly, this can be quite relevant in the context he is working in, since certain environmental risks have been underrated and hushed up for many years.

Beck deprecates the importance of statistical calculations of risks because risks are always evaluated in relation to political and moral norms. Beck does, nevertheless, give an example where he considers a risk-claim to be exaggerated, namely the Brent Spar-conflict. But here he blames Greenpeace, not the media, for the exaggeration. As a parallel to framing theory, there is much importance attached to the influence of semantics and symbols in Beck's theory; and he explains that experts and mass media can get a key position in society by defining risks. It is therefore surprising that he pays so little attention to how the media handle and select this means of power.

Mary Douglas tells us that what we fear most are the things that disturb our sense of the order of nature. Her studies are based on tribal societies where modern mass media are nonexistent. Subsequently, she has tried to apply the same theories to modern societies, together with Aaron Wildavsky. The analysis of the environment protection movement performed by these two anthropologists has been interpreted as a claim that these organizations create fictive risks in order to consolidate their internal organization. In a reply to this criticism, Douglas vehemently rejects this interpretation, and she even goes as far as to completely deny that humans are liable to construct fictive risks. She reveals a great insight in the political significance of who gets the blame for mishaps, but accidents are always real to Douglas. She is ambiguous on the question of whether a person can gain advantage by exaggerating or constructing dangers. People are not good at evaluating risks and making rational choices based on small probabilities. The choice of which risks to accept and which to combat is a social process depending on the social organization. Douglas and Wildavsky do not consider the role of mass media in this selection process.

Psychologist Karl Dake has defined four different types of orienting dispositions based on Mary Douglas' group/grid model of social organization: hierarchical, individualist, egalitarian, and fatalist. These dispositions bias people in the way they perceive different types of risks. Hierarchically oriented persons are most concerned with dangers connected with social deviance and crime. Individualists support economic liberalism and fear those risks that threaten the market economy. What egalitarians fear most is technological risks that threaten the environment. Finally, the fatalists are not very concerned about risks at all. Statistical investigations find that it is difficult to divide individuals into these categories. Nevertheless, the statistics find a small, yet significant, correlation that largely supports the predicted tendencies.

Based on risk sociology, Maarten Hajer has submitted the environmental debate to a discourse analysis à la Foucault. According to this theory, the discursive order is defined by story lines which provide the frame of reference and define the moral order of the debate. The story lines determine which objects are communicable in a given culture. Hence, social actors can exercise power if they succeed in defining the story lines. The mass media are only mentioned cursorily, even in Hajer's discourse analyses. Apparently, he only sees the media as a passive service organ for the communication of social actors, while the role of journalists as social actors is only mentioned in a parenthesis.

Deviance Sociology

The sociology of deviance is a study of how society defines certain persons, phenomena or behaviors as deviant and dangerous. The dangerous is thus a social construct. Society can control unwanted behaviors by defining them as sinful or sick. Whoever has success in defining the norms of what is considered deviant and dangerous has thus gained a key position in the social power apparatus. Sometimes, a social deviance is considered so dangerous that it must be combated with the most draconian means. Such a manifestation of exaggerated fear is called a witch-hunt or moral panic. These persecutions have been compared with magic rituals in accordance with Mary Douglas' theory.

In modern society, there is a fierce competition for defining what is dangerous to society. Numerous organizations and lobbying groups compete for setting the agenda for the discussion of social problems in order to get more resources for their particular cause. This has very aptly been called the social problems marketplace. Throughout the times, various professions like priests, lawyers, psychologists, psychiatrists, neurologists, etc. have had monopoly on making statements about certain dangerous deviancies. Thereby they gain power and influence through what has been called issue ownership. Many sociologists have described how certain social problems get inflated to hysterical proportions because of the way they are exposed in the media. Media-created fears have made people change their lifestyles, have changed the nature of social policies and undermined the process of justice.

Evaluation of Media Claims

A strict constructionist would not allow any evaluation of media claims, no matter how outrageous they may be. We need a more pragmatic social analysis. When comparing risks, we may look for support in various natural sciences, such as statistics. Whatever method we use for evaluating risks and dangers, we have to accept a certain inaccuracy and admit that there are disagreements on which measures to use. This inaccuracy means that we can only detect big distortions in the media, not small distortions. Not seldom, however, the exaggerations or downplayings in the media are so gross that they will be obvious to everybody.

Risk analysis is a research tradition based on statistics, psychology and sociology. Risk analysts have found that experts evaluate risks on the basis of statistical criteria, while lay people tend to base their evaluation on political and moral criteria and on how individual risks affect people. The characteristics of different risks have been divided into two main factors according to the so-called psychometric model:

— *Factor 1* comprises risks that are unknown to the persons affected, unknown to science, new, involuntary, and with slow effect.

— *Factor 2* characterizes risks that have fatal, dreaded and catastrophic consequences as well as consequences for future generations.

It has been found that people's fear and their demand for risk-reducing intervention is influenced much more by factor 2 than by factor 1. Risk analysts have also adopted Dake's cultural theory of orienting dispositions.

Paul Slovic has identified a group consisting mainly of white men who consider many risks less serious than the rest of the population do. This group is characterized as mainly hierarchical and individualistically oriented. On the basis of both the psychometric and the cultural model, Slovic concludes that people's emotional response is primary to their attitude towards risks, and that their evaluation of advantages and disadvantages of risky activities is secondary and at least partially determined thereby.

It is also important to what degree people have trust in the organizations or authorities that are supposed to control risks. It is noteworthy, that trust is easier to break down than to build up. Sources of bad news are regarded as more trustworthy than sources of reassurance. A single investigation finding that a certain activity is risky has more impact than a large number of investigations finding no risk.

Risk analysts have set up a model of how the social effects of a risk are amplified or attenuated when channeled through the different units of society. The direct effect of the risk factor in terms of damage or exposure to danger has influence on people's risk perception directly as well as through the mass media. The risk perception so formed gives rise to individual as well as collective reactions, which may have a range of cultural and socioeconomic consequences. These consequences often feed back on the risk factor with the effect that it is either decreased or increased.

People tend to evaluate the probability associated with a risk on the basis of the amount of information they receive about the risk factor. The perception of a risk is thus shaped by the amount of media coverage and the vividness of this information. The media coverage is determined by factors such as causality, responsibility and blame, according to agenda setting research.

Framing also has a strong effect. For example, people's attitude towards a risk or danger depends on whether it has been described in strictly scientific and statistical terms, or the media have focused on uncertainty, economy, health, environment, who is affected, justice, equality, etc.Scholars of risk communication tell us that it is important how the responsible authorities inform the population about risks. The population should be kept informed about the newest knowledge about technological risks and the efforts to reduce these risks in order to build up trust. It is necessary to bridge the gap between technical descriptions and people's personal perception of security.

An information vacuum is created if the responsible organizations ignore or deny a risk. The population, the media, and grassroots organizations will seek to fill this vacuum with information from other sources. The lack of trust that arises leads to an amplification of the conflict with increased media coverage and excessive fear as a result. This may often force the authorities to implement quite drastic measures against the risk that they originally tried to downplay. The handling of the mad cow disease by the British government is a good example of how a problem that the authorities originally denied developed into a major moral panic which in the end forced the society to spend enormous amounts of money on fighting the problem. In conclusion, the study of risk communication provides part of the explanation of what makes the population and the media overreact to certain risks.

Some studies have indicated that the viewing of fear-provoking television programs cultivates authoritarianism. The concept of authoritarianismhas been widely used and studied in social psychology for half a century. Unfortunately, this concept is strongly criticized for being vaguely defined and politically biased. Therefore, the cultural r/k theory is preferred here as an alternative to the theory of authoritarianism.

With a theoretical basis in cultural selection theory, the r/k theory avoids the political bias and accusations of psychopathology that lies implicitly in the diagnosis of authoritarianism. The cultural r/k scale, which may be seen as a replacement for the authoritarianism scale, is applicable not only to individuals, but also to entire cultures and cultural products.

A culture and its population will, according to this theory, adapt to the environment in which the society finds itself and, more specifically, to the need for defense against factors that threaten the nation or social group. The perception of a bellicose neighbor state as a security threat will give rise to a kind of psychological armament in the citizens who see their nation or tribe as threatened. The solidarity and feeling of group identity will be strengthened. It has been discovered that these social psychological reactions give rise to a whole series of emergent cultural phenomena.

The political structure will be more hierarchical because people feel the need for a strong leader. The ideology will go in the direction of saying that individuals exist for the sake of the society, rather than vice versa. Religious life will be stricter. Discipline will be harsh and the tolerance for deviants will go down. Sexual morals will also be stricter, and the birthrate will go up. Interestingly, it has been found that these cultural changes are also reflected in the artistic production. Architecture, pictorial art, fiction, and even music becomes more formalistic, embellished and perfectionist so as to achieve a cognitive congruence between the art and the social system where political and religious leaders have a grandiose and majestic status.

A culture that exhibits these characteristics is called regal. The opposite tendencies are called kalyptic. A kalyptic culture is typified by peacefulness, tolerance and individualism. You may imagine a continuous r/k scale going from the extremely regal to the extremely kalyptic, where most cultures and their individual members fluctuate somewhere around the middle of this scale.

Any danger that is perceived as threatening to the social order and to the nation as a whole can have a regal influence. This effect has been exploited by despots throughout history who have created witch-hunts and fictitious enemies in order to boost social solidarity and thereby consolidate their dwindling power.

The regal development not only makes a social group better armed to resist violent attacks, but also more likely to initiate a violent conflict. A culture will drift in the kalyptic direction in the absence of any serious threats to the nation and to the social order. People will not accept a tyrannical rule when nothing legitimizes the call for a strong leadership and nothing justifies the requirement that people make great sacrifices for the sake of their nation.

Applying the cultural r/k theory to our analysis of the mass media, we find that excessive fear mongering can have far-reaching consequences if it makes people see their society as constantly endangered. As mentioned above in the discussion of framing effects, the intense focus on crime reporting and the personalized framing of these reports gives the audience the impression that crimes are caused by moral defects in individuals or by an ineffective penal system. The consequence is that ever more resources are spent on ineffective punitive measures and less on the more effective preventive measures.

These political consequences of the intense media focus on crime and danger are in agreement with the predictions of the cultural r/k theory, though they may be explained without the use of this theory. However, the predictions of the r/k theory are more farreaching. The more the media cultivate the fear of crimes and other dangers that threaten the social order, the more the culture develops in the regal direction. This is likely to influence not only the crime policy, but to lead to lower tolerance towards all kinds of minorities, more xenophobia, and a tougher foreign policy.

Now that we have analyzed several paradigms for what they have to say about the mass media, it is time to assemble the jigsaw puzzle into a coherent model. Economic theory can clarify the effect of unrestrained competition on the media market. While the immediate expectation of economists is that free competition leads to optimization, a more thorough analysis shows that this belief does not hold for the media market.

A mild degree of competition may lead to improved quality and diversity, but excessive competition between commercial media has been found theoretically as well as empirically to lead to wasteful duplication of the most popular entertainment genres rather than to a diversity of genres. Economists are reluctant to use any other measure of quality than diversity of genres, but this is indeed a poor measure of quality. One model even suggests a negative relationship between diversity and quality; and as the cultivation studies show, a diversity of genres does not guarantee a diversity of messages.

The commercial media avoid controversial issues. The distinctions between advertisements, news and entertainment are blurred. And audience groups with less spending money are not considered. The result of excessive competition, one may conclude, is a choice of very similar sensationalist and entertaining programs with low production costs and low informational value. This benefits neither consumers nor advertisers.

Journalists and editors often deplore this development and try to improve the quality of their media by advocating principles of journalistic standards and media ethics. These efforts have little effect, however, because the effects of the economic market forces are able to override the lower level effects of journalistic selection, according to cultural selection theory.

Media studies clearly show the consequences of strong competition between the mass media. The media are trying to generate a sense of personal proximity. Political disagreements are presented as a clash between personalities rather than between ideological principles. The stories often appeal to the emotions rather than to the intellect.

Advertisers prefer soft entertainment and shun controversy. Relaxing entertainment may not suffice for attracting the attention of viewers or readers, however. In order to survive in the competition for attention, the media often turn to emotional and attention-catching subjects like crime, fear, danger, and of course sex and gossip. There is a remarkable consistency among different scientific disciplines in the finding that certain topics like these are used repeatedly in the media for catching attention. The discipline of evolutionary psychology even gives a theoretical reason why these topics catch our attention.

The fact that topics relating to fear and danger have such a prominent place in the media demands special attention. Risk sociology tells us that personal dispositions may influence which types of risks people fear most. The discipline of risk analysis tells us that people's evaluation of risks is determined by emotional factors rather than by statistical probabilities.

Certain risks have a greater emotional impact than others, and studies of risk communication adds the finding that it makes a big difference whether information about a certain risk is communicated in a way that makes people feel that the authorities are in control of the situation or not. These findings all add up to an understanding of the sociological discovery that people often fear the wrong things and take drastic precautions against the most unlikely dangers while ignoring other much more serious risks. These effects are of course mirrored and amplified by the media.

The sociology of deviance has discovered that certain professionals and organizations can gain power by defining a danger, making people afraid of it, and at the same time claiming their expertise in fighting this danger. This position is so attractive that numerous interest groups are competing fiercely for gaining recognition for their particular social problem, and their particular definition of it, and having it placed high on the media agenda. The media may find it quite profitable to cooperate with such an interest group and run a highly emotional and attention-catching campaign about a particular social problem. Exaggerations are the norm rather than the exception here, and the situation may soon develop into a moral panic or witchhunt.

Now that we have identified some of the most important factors that influence the form and contents of the mass media, it is time to analyze how these media affect the viewers, listeners, and readers. The fact that the most attention-catching topics have such a prominent place in the media will inevitably have a strong effect according to the theories of agendasetting, priming, and cultivation.

The strong focus on topics involving fear and danger in the media agenda will also place these topics high on the political agenda. A politician wanting re-election cannot ignore a sensational media campaign or moral panic. Even in the rare case where a politician can resist the emotional appeal of the media and see the hard facts behind the stories, he or she still has to "do something" to satisfy the public opinion.

The consequence is that laws about problems with a high

media-appeal may be changed frequently without a rational analysis. Another topic, which is often used for catching attention, is, obviously, sex. Stories about sex may be either positive ("sex is good") or negative ("sex is bad and dangerous"). Both types of stories are equally good for catching attention.

The high prominence of sex on the agenda may thus influence the sexual morals of the society in either the liberal or the restrictive direction, depending on which kind of stories fit best into the agenda of the time. Economic considerations influence not only the subject matter of media stories, but also the form. Commercial media prefer to present issues in a personalized way. Ideological disagreements are presented as conflicts between persons. Likewise, social problems are explained by presenting examples of persons who are afflicted by these problems. Such stories appeal more to the emotions than to the intellect. Complicated explanations are avoided. Stories, which cannot be presented in this personalized frame, are often simply not told. The consequence of this form of presentation can be predicted from the theory of framing.

The framing of a story determines the causal understanding and attribution of blame for a particular problem. Social problems are most likely blamed on individual persons when framed in a personalized manner. Since the deeper structural causes of the problems are seldom explained, the likely political consequence is scapegoating, but not solution of the problems. The incessant media focus on fear, danger, crime and disaster make people perceive the world as a gloomy and dangerous place.

The psychological reaction to this perception may be predicted from the cultural r/k theory. If the entire nation, and not only individuals, are perceived as endangered, then this "mean world syndrome" will foster the kind of social climate that is commonly known as authoritarian. The culture will become more punitive, intolerant, hierarchical and bellicose. Interestingly, the framing theory leads to some of the same predictions, but based on a different mechanism. We thus have two different mechanisms leading in approximately the same direction. These two mechanisms are not mutually exclusive, but more likely to supplement each other.

The mass media are influenced by several factors: Media owners define the overall editorial policy of a medium. Economic factors determine the amount of journalistic investigation and cultural production that can be afforded. A highly competitive market with wasteful duplication of the most popular genres leaves few economic resources to spend on heightening the quality of each program.

Economic considerations may force the media to deploy an attention-catching strategy by emphasizing entertainment, emotional and personalized stories, sex, violence, gossip, etc. Economy determines the influence of advertisers and sponsors on the types of programs and stories that are being published.

Sponsors also have an influence through sponsored cultural events and sports events that may not take place unless they are profitable to the sponsors. The news are obtained from sources such as politicians, opinion leaders, experts, professionals, police, organizations, and ordinary people who happen to be involved in a newsworthy situation.

These sources can influence the media, not only through the stories they tell, but also by rewarding or punishing certain media by providing or withholding desired information. The editors and journalists who produce stories obviously have an influence through their personal engagement as well as their professional, ideological and ethical principles.

Technology determines how many media channels we can have and which formats are possible and attractive. Government regulation may impose additional ethical principles such as fairness requirements and public service obligations.

All these factors influence the form and contents of the media products. However, the most important implication is that the degree of economic competition between the mass media is a meta-factor, which determines the weight of the other factors. A strongly competitive market situation may force the media producers to give more weight to considerations of attention-catching and to the wishes of the advertisers and less weight to ideology and ethics.

Ideals of fairness, relevance, and thorough investigative journalism have little influence when fierce economic competition drains the media organizations of resources and forces them to compete on attention-catching stories and entertainment. Quality media that refuse to compete on these premises may simply perish unless they can rely on noncommercial sources of funding.

The media are conveying and influencing the public opinion, which in turn determines the democratic elections. The influence of the media works not only through voters' opinions.

Everybody in society is influenced by the media, including politicians, opinion leaders, journalists, editors, and whoever may have the role of news sources. Furthermore, the media are influencing the criteria by which voters evaluate political candidates by means of agendasetting, priming and framing.

The impact of recent technological innovations on the media market has often been discussed. Some commentators have claimed that pay-per-view technologies can correct the market failures inherent in advertisement-based media. But even in the unlikely event that a commercial supplier will offer a pay-per-view news channel free of advertisements, sponsoring and product placement, there will still be an economic influence from the owner.

Tabloid newspapers sold from newsstands are known to produce more attention-catching headlines than subscription-based broadsheet newspapers, because they need to attract impulse buyers every day. A pay-per-view based supplier of TV or internet news will be likely to use a similar strategy. The increase in the number of channels and distribution methods will only increase the competition for attention further. The Internet has made dissemination of information so cheap that non-commercial suppliers of information can afford to make their services available world-vide. This does not reduce the costs of investigative journalism; neither does it reduce the competition for attention, but at least it opens up more possibilities for a news-supply that is less influenced by economic interests.

Media and E-democracy

The reality around that world is that established media brands are the number one online providers of political news and information - at least in terms of users. Therefore, the future of e-democracy relies in large part on how the media takes advantage of the two- nature of the Internet versus their traditional one-way communication models.

One of the roles of the media has traditionally been to provide the general public with information about the activities of public authorities. Increasingly, however, such information is made directly available to the general public on official web sites. This is at first sight a positive development serving the right of the public to access information. The question arises, however, of what role remains for the media?

Once, they used to be a unique link between public authorities and the citizen, while now they may become marginalised. It seems obvious that the media should continue to extract information from the public sector, since there is no guarantee that the information provided by public authorities on their own initiative is objective and exhaustive. Furthermore, it may be argued that the amount of available information makes "filtering" and interpretation even more necessary than before. No one seems to be better placed than independent media to correct misleading official information. The media should therefore act as an independent observer of public authorities and their information policy, highlighting what is really newsworthy and criticising what could be done better.

The advice of media professionals can also be valuable when it comes to deciding how information on public web sites is structured. Public documents should for example be presented in a transparent and easily accessible manner facilitating the work of media professionals and others who follow the activities of public authorities.

It is commonplace to say that the media reflect public opinion. New technical possibilities allow the media to collect the views of the public in a much more direct way than before. Conducting an on-line vote with the help of the Internet is technically fairly easy and many on-line media invite the public to voice their opinion on certain topics, for example by simply clicking a "yes" or "no" button in answer to particular questions.

The question arises, however, whether the media have developed any guidelines on how to conduct and present the results of such on-line votes. For the sake of fairness and transparency, the media might, for example, provide information on the composition of the sample which would allow the audience to judge to what extent it is representative.

Furthermore, it might be interesting to know if the media present the results of such votes to decision-makers, requesting a reaction.

There is nothing new about the fact that the media offer

the public the possibility of engaging in a discussion about public affairs. This has been done in the past in the form of letters to the editor, talkshows on radio and television, etc.

New technologies open up new possibilities in this respect. Many on- line media invite readers to comment on stories or to provide input in chat-sessions or discussion fora on topical issues.

Several questions can be raised in this respect. Firstly, whether the media should issue any guidelines to participants in on-line debates regarding respect for the law and ethical principles. Secondly, whether the debates should be moderated and, in the affirmative, whether they should be premoderated or postmoderated.

Premoderation may, in particular, be necessary when sensitive topics are being discussed or where children are encouraged to take part. Thirdly, whether participants should be allowed to hide their identity. In addition to these questions, which the media will first and foremost decide for themselves, there is the issue of legal responsibility for content of on-line debates. Over and above these issues, which are immediately linked to the organisation of on-line debates, there is the question of what is done with the results.

The media may have an important role to play in promoting democratic practices. This can be done, for example, by encouraging participation in elections and referenda and devoting special attention to such democratic processes. This could also involve providing information to voters about the democratic system that they belong to. In the context of the information society, this would mean that the media follow closely new developments aimed at increasing democratic participation in decision-making about public affairs. Where no such developments are taking place, the media could furthermore enquire why this is the case.

The media may also pay special attention to the phenomenon of diminished interest in public affairs and suggest ways for public authorities and politicians to involve the general public to a greater extent than before. More public interest and involvement will also ultimately be beneficial to the media themselves, at least as regards the sustainability of serious reporting about politics, the economy, etc.

The media should, furthermore, pay special attention to the views, concerns and situation of marginalised or excluded parts of society. Such a moral obligation is to be found in many ethical codes and is respected in practice by a large number of media professionals. This may be particularly urgent in the context of the information society, where new forms of social exclusion may arise. People without access to the Internet or lacking skills in using the Internet may effectively be worse off than before from a democratic point of view.

5

Media and Socio-Economic Development

Mass media development exhibited stronger causal relationships with both economic and political development than social and telecommunication development. An independent media can boost economic development by promoting good governance and empowering citizens. It can make economies function better. There are many examples of this around the world. In Colombia, for example, a couple of years ago, a local TV station broadcast a video that showed a corrupt public official bribing an opposition Member of Congress. Others reported that he was smuggling arms to Colombian guerrillas, and he was soon dismissed.

There are empirical studies that show how public health efforts can be improved. Women's access to the media has been associated with better health and fertility outcomes even after accounting for income and education levels. Increasingly, the work of governments, international organizations, communities, and citizens around the world is geared toward promoting transparency. Information or transparency is an essential ingredient of any initiative designed to enhance the accountability of economic and political actors.

People care about their reputations, and media attention

can provide strong incentives for changing behavior. Reputational penalties and rewards can be powerful in ensuring accountability toward constituents. Greater transparency supported by the media can convince people to follow rules and laws set down by government, but it can do much more. It can ensure that people behave in socially responsible ways even in the absence of laws or when laws are weak and unenforceable.

There is an undeniable symbiotic relationship between media, government, and business. This is evident if one considers that media survival depends on its net revenue, which comes not just from consumers of news, but which is dependent on advertising revenues, on government subsidies, fees, or taxes. And moreover, the regulatory environment in which it operates is determined by government.

How independent the industry is affects its quality. More independent media tend to produce more reliable and better analysis. Of course, quality is also affected by training and by the sources of checks and balances on the media itself.

Media and Political Development

One of the first analyses of the importance of communication in the political development process was provided by L.W. Pye in 1956. From his perspective, communication in developing nations performed a key function in structuring the political process. Based on case studies, he argued that the influence of communication on political structure dif-fered in urban and rural areas.

Pye noted that the Western-style mass media in urban areas tended to cover the political process from a national perspective, thus enhancing a sense of nationalism and support for developing political institutions. In more rural areas, where word of mouth was still the predominant form of communication, villagers remained oriented to local events, their opinions on which were influenced by informal opinion leaders. The urban frames of reference of newspapers had little meaning to villagers, when they were read to them in their villages.

S.M. Lipset focused on the relationship between economic development and the legitimacy of political systems. Lipset hypothesized that demo-cratic systems of government were more likely to flourish in wealthier nations, because only in them could citizens be expected to participate intelligently in the political process and avoid the appeals of demagogic authoritarian leaders. A country divided between a large impoverished mass and a small wealthy elite would likely result in political systems based on oligarchy or tyranny, according to Lipset.

Lipset provided correlational evidence that supported this hypothesis for Latin American, European, and other English-speaking nations. Stable democracies in these regions were higher than unstable democracies or dictatorships on all the main "indicators of wealth," as Lipset referred to them: per capita income, doctors, motor vehicles, telephones, radios, and newspapers per 1,000 people. Urbanization, literacy, school enrollment, per capita energy consumption, and the percentage of nonagricultural workers were also higher in the countries with stable democratic regimes.

Similarly, P. Cutright tested the proposition that social, economic, commun-ication, and political development were interrelated. To create an index of political development, Cutright assigned scores to 76 nations from 1940 to 1961 based on the degree of competition present among political parties and in elections of chief executives. Communication development, which was measured by an index of daily newspapers per 1,000 people, newsprint consumption, telephones, and pieces of domestic mail per capita, was the strongest predictor of political development, followed by degree of urbanization, school enrollment, and the percentage of the labor force engaged in agricultural work.

K.W. Deutsch conducted one of the first studies to measure communication flow among countries. His analysis of first-class mail flow among 48 countries prior to WW II showed that more than 75 percent of them received more letters from abroad than they sent. In the seven most industrialized countries, however, this ratio was reversed. Ratios of local to non-local mail also tended to decrease within larger US cities, as did ratios for non-local to foreign mail. Such national measures of "intake-output ratios," according to Deutsch, served as indicators of integration among countries.

These and other studies generated considerable research, from which emerged the political development paradigm which posited that an array of socioeconomic variables, once they reached certain levels, would lead to more democratic and stable political regimes. The practical implications of this research for guiding the development aid programs of world powers and the UN in developing countries generated considerable debate in the 1960s. H.J. Wiarda summarized the issues this way:

> The political development paradigm was derived from Western experience and therefore was of limited usefulness in non-Western areas. As a result, the optimum outcome of political development was too often narrowly defined in terms of Western-style voting participation rather than a broader concern for political and civil freedoms.
>
> The timing and sequences of political development stages may differ between developed and less developed nations or from region to region.
>
> The complex webs of interdependencies among nations, which may affect their economic and political development, were not sufficiently investigated.
>
> The roles indigenous cultural or social institutions could

> play in promoting change and helping bridge the gap during the transition from traditional to modern societies were not studied. Some formulations of the political de-velopment paradigm suggested that those from Western countries should replace indigenous cultural or social institutions.

Some political scientists, in fact, argued that developing democratic political institutions too swiftly could hinder economic development. A proponent of this view was S.P Huntington, who stated that political democracy may be a luxury that developing nations could not afford. He argued that the pressures of participatory democracy could quickly overwhelm the political institutions of developing countries, which tended to be fragile to begin with, thereby magnifying the forces of instability. Therefore, more authoritarian regimes were better able to cope with the stresses of economic development. Taken as a whole, the evidence concerning the political development paradigm was decidedly inconsistent.

L. Sirowy and Inkeles reviewed studies that examined the economic consequences of different types of political regimes. Of the 13 studies they examined, three supported the conclusion that democracy may hinder economic develop-ment, six reported no relationship between democracy and economic growth, and four indicated a conditional relationship. Furthermore, half of another 12 studies indicated that democratic regimes actually reduced economic inequality or had no effect, while the other half suggested an inverse relationship between the two indicators.

Media and Communication Development

An important focus of research in the communication field in the 1950s and 1960s was how mass media technology could be used to stimulate and modernize the econo-mies and political systems of developing countries. The development paradigm that evolved from this research posited that indigenous people needed to abandon their trad-itional ways of thinking and life on subsistence farms to participate in the cash sector of the economy. The quickest and most effective way of bringing this about was argued to be information campaigns disseminated via the mass media.

By the far the most influential early study shaping the development communication paradigm was undertaken in the Middle East by Daniel Lerner. Lerner theorized that economic and political development resulted from a process that began when a country's population was about 10 percent urbanized. At that point, mass media and literacy growth interacted in a "multiplier effect" to produce a critical mass of citizens with "mobile personalities" who desire to participate in the economic and political life of their country. When a critical mass of such citizens is reached, which he predicted to be at about 25 percent urbanization, then economic development takes off, ultimately resulting in a democratic political regime, which Lerner termed the "crowning glory" of the process.

His secondary analysis of census data from Turkey, Lebanon, Egypt, Syria, Jordan, and Iran indicated that the percent voting in these countries was highly correlated with degree of urbanization, literacy, and media consumption. Survey results showed that "transitionals," those who were in the process of moving from traditional to more modern lifestyles, tended to have most recently moved from a rural to urban homes, had the highest exposure to media, and the most understanding and empathy for the role of the media. Furthermore, transitionals in the six countries had the highest recall of inter-national news items, the greatest variety of opinions, and were most likely to believe that they could influence national problems.

Correlational evidence appeared to support the D. Lerner model of economic and political modernization. Per capita income, proportion of adults literate, and daily news-paper circulation, as derived from 1959 UNESCO data on 85 countries by R.B. Nixon, were strongly correlated with degree of press freedom as rated by the International Press Institute.

A regression analysis by R. Farace and L. Donohew showed that press control, newspaper circulation, and radio receivers per 100 people were significantly predicted by illiteracy rates, per capita income, ideological orientation of the country, population, life expectancy, and the legislative-executive structure in 115 countries in 1962. Economic and media development indices dominated in a factor analysis by Farace of 54 political, economic, and cultural indicators in 109 countries in 1964. A later analysis by Farace demonstrated that six distinct regional patterns existed among this group of indicators of national development.

However, causal analyses testing the Lerner model produced mixed results. H.R. Alker's path analysis of aggregate national data from the early 1960s showed that urbanization predicted literacy and media development, while literacy tended to predict economic and political participation indirectly through media development. Another path analysis by D.J. McCrone and C.F. Cnudde tested six alternative models of the basic vari-ables in the Lerner model. The best causal fit to their data was one in which urbanization leads to education, which directly predicted communication development, which in turn led to higher voting participation.

Time series analyses provided stronger evidence on the Lerner model. Based on cross-lagged correlations from UN data from 1951 through 1961, W. Schramm and L. Ruggels concluded that per capita income and urbanization affected literacy in early stages of development more than the reverse case. Yet the causal relationships among per capita income, urbanization, literacy, and indicators of newspaper and radio development were not clear in their analysis.

G.R. Winham tested the Lerner model by utilizing time-series data on 10-year intervals in the United States from 1790. An index of political development was created for each 10-year period from a sum of scores for minority parties in the US Congress and a directly elected chief executive with a vote participation multiplier. Communications development was operationalized as an index of post office expenditures, total number of newspapers, and periodicals, as well as telephones, radios and television per capita. Time-lagged correlations indicated that communications were a stronger predictor of political development than vice versa. The same was found for the relationship between political development and education, but only after a 20-year lag. On the other hand, the US data indicated that communications development may precede urbanization, contrary to the Lerner model.

As with the political development paradigm, a reassessment of the commun-ication developmental paradigm among communication scholars began in the late 1960s. Also in part motivated by the policy implications of the research, the debate about the develop-ment communication paradigm produced criticism similar to that of the political develop-ment paradigm. According to N. Jayaweera, these criticisms included:

> Development includes more than economic growth in a country, but requires equal distribution of wealth also.
>
> Promotion of political participation at the national and local levels, educational opportunities, civil liberties, as well as factors pertaining to quality of life, should also be important goals of development communication.
>
> The development communication paradigm tended to replicate the individualism and materialism of the Western society. Instead, communication campaigns should be conducted within the context of the culture, customs, and values of the people.

In reality, after a decade of heavy investment in the mass media infrastructures of de-veloping nations, the results were mixed in the 1970s. In 1975, E. Sathre provided evidence that in the previous 10 years, the GNP in developing countries had increased more than 50 percent, exports to them were up 124 percent, nonagricultural employment had improved to 52 percent, and food production had grown to 30 percent, among other indicators. During the same period of time, mass media development had also signifi-cantly increased in these countries, including a 100 million more radio receivers.

However, while overall economic development did increase in real terms, the gap between rich and poor countries grew, population rates continued to skyrocket, unem-ployment rose, and the quality of life indicators improved only for those of the highest socio-economic status. Moreover, economic development had not necessarily lead to political stability and democracy, as many of the newly created democracies during the 1960s were replaced by military dictatorships or one-party regimes. Lerner's explanation for these developments was that the "want/get" ratios among the populations of developing countries had become so disproportionate that the "revolution of rising expectations" predicted by the development communication paradigm had resulted instead in a "revolution of rising frustrations."

Early studies of both the political development and develop communication para-digms were generally not adequate to test the hypothesized causal relationships among indicators. Most had to utilize either cross-sectional data or time series of short duration, because organizations such as the World Bank and UNESCO had just begun compiling yearly development indicator statistics in the 1960s. Furthermore, statistical techniques for assessing causality among indicators were not yet highly developed, as well as the computer software and hardware necessary to perform them. Evidence from early studies of both paradigms, therefore, should be replicated, utilizing the greater variety of time series of longer duration now available.

Another consideration is the extent to which the evidence regarding the political development and communication development paradigms is historically bound. The studies of both paradigms conducted in the 1960-1970 era, when the development in most countries had been underway for only about a decade. Increases in economic and political development might well have lagged behind increases in these socioeconomic indicators by long periods of time. Moreover, both economic and political stability in developing countries might also take varying lengths of time to achieve, preceded by irregularly occurring periods of disruption. Only time-series data of long duration can be used to assess the lag between stimulus and response in this way.

Surprisingly few macro-level studies, however, have been published regarding the political development and development communication paradigms after the 1970s. Recently, however, the new struggling democracies in Eastern Europe and the introduction of new communication technologies with their economic and political impli-cations have resulted in renewed interest in this area of research. Many of these studies have used considerably broadened con-ceptualizations of both economic and political development.

J. Fedderke and Klitgaard found that GDP per capita was associated with greater civil and political rights, when measured by a number of socioeconomic time series up to 25 years in length for as many as 118 countries. GDP per capita was also significantly associated with higher levels of education, greater likelihood of a market economy, a higher percentage of the population exposed to modernizing influences, and greater consumption of the news media. In a multivariate analysis, political rights proved to be the strongest predictor of per capita GDP.

S.Borner, A. Brunetti and B. Weder noted that most previous operationalizations of democracy in studies of economic development have focused on the existence or fairness of elections, competition among political parties, or the freedom of opposition groups to operate. But such dimensions of democracy, they argued, are of low relevance to inves-tors in the economies of developing countries who are more concerned with the uncertainties posed by political instability in both democratic and authoritarian regimes.

Accordingly, Borner et al. designed a measure of political credibility to tap the degree of uncertainty arising from state actions. Entrepreneurs operating in developing countries were sent questionnaires asking them how regularly they had to cope with unexpected laws and policy changes and the extent to which governments stick to an-nounced major policies in the countries in which they operated. Respondents indicated that these factors were more important in their investment decisions than high transaction costs or even corruption. In 10 developing countries, political credibility proved to be more highly correlated with economic growth than other frequently used measures of democracy.

A number of studies have explored the relevance of telecommunication develop-ment to political and economic development. Using data from 45 countries, A.P. Hardy found that per capita GDP and the number of telephones per capita mutually influenced each other between 1960 and 1973, based on time-lagged offsets of one year. Similarly, F.J. Cronin, E.BN. Parker, E.K. Colleran and M.A. Gold's analysis of 31 years of US data from 1958 through 1988 showed a two-way effect between telecommunications investment and overall economic growth, based on two-year lag intervals. Using data from 23 countries from 1975 to 1991 from several sources, J. Zhu's pooled time-series analysis showed that the previous year's telephone development but not radio or television was a significant predictor of GNP. But with a three-year lag, television and radio penetration also became significant predictors of GNP.

The Japanese Johoka Shakai approach to the study of development commun-ication has taken into account the role of new media technology. As Y. Ito described it, johoka shakai translated means "informationalized society," as opposed to kogyoka shakai, or "industrialized society." The Johoka Index was composed of a simple, summed index of indicators in four categories:

— amount of information (telephone calls per person per year, newspaper circulation, books read per 1000 people, and population density);

— distribution of communication media (telephone receivers per 100 people, radios and television sets per 100 households);

— quality of information activities (proportion of service workers in labor population and proportion of students in total appropriate age group;

— the information ratio of each country (a ratio of household expenditures for information-related activities to total expenditures)

The first analyses in the 1970s showed that each of the five major industrialized societies–US, Japan, UK, West Germany, and France–had significantly increased on all the Johoka Index measures between 1953 and 1975. While the United States was the most informationalized society throughout this period, Japan's growth, according to the Johoka Index measures, was steepest, resulting in the country being ranked No. 2 ahead of the United Kingdom, West Germany and France, respectively, by the late 1960s. Also, the information ratio index was highly correlated with per capita income in a broader sample of developed and developing nations.

H.S Dorick and G. Wang argued that development communications has been replaced in this era by "development informationization." Using measures from mea-sures the Johoka Index, the results showed that telephone and computer/data terminal penetration grew significantly between 1970 and 1980, but the rate of penetration was greater in richer than poorer countries. Differences in mass media penetration rates among nations were less dramatic compare to telecommunications, computers, and data terminals. While television and radio diffusion slowed in more developed countries in the 1970s, as they reached saturation levels, their penetration rates continued to grow in the less developed countries, with the exception of newspaper circulation per 1000 people.

Among the eight most highly industrialized nations, Dorick and Wang's analysis showed that by 1980 the information sectors constituted at least 40 percent of their work forces, while wide differences existed in this proportion among less wealthier nations. The average percentage contribution of the information sectors to the GDP per capita of wealthier nations rose from 43 percent in 1980 to 65 percent in 1988. A less impressive contribution by the information sector to GDP per capita was evidenced for middle-level countries, while none was apparent among those with the lowest incomes.

Media and Cultural Development

Culture is the group linked by more or less formalized ways of thinking, feeling and acting which, learnt and shared by a plurality of persons, serve in both an objective and symbolic way, to constitute those persons in a particular and distinct collective. Culture singularizes human groups and merges identities together, but, at the same time, it places these groups in relation to the rest of society. The public nature of culture is expressed in manifestations such as the arts, customs, the social system, language or religion.

Cultural diversity is recognized externally and internally, both by the prevailing institutions of civil society and by the awareness of the group itself as different to the whole in some expressions. However, the concept of cultural diversity does not appear to be properly defined. Even though language is a diversifying element of special importance, a unanimous appraisal of other elements which distinguish one culture from another is not to be found.

The media have become the chief transmitters of culture. The traditional showcases of culture—museums, theatres, art galleries or libraries —have handed over part of their functions to the cinema screens, television or computers; media where culture has greater distribution and scope, since the images reach broader, more heterogeneous and widespread audiences. The cultural function of the audiovisual industry is not only developed by the broadcasting of eminently cultural issues; news programmes, fiction series and films, video games or game programmes, for example, also display cultural manifestations that reinforce identities, show diversity in social situations and distinguish the ways of thinking and feeling of the social groups included in a community.

The audiovisual sector is, therefore, one more source of cultural creativity. The audiovisual sector is seen as closely linked to other cultural activities, such as literature or art. The express mention of audiovisual production in art is significant: it underlines how the audiovisual sector is a cultural manifestation, distancing itself from a purely commercial approach. The leading role which will be played by cinema, television and multimedia communication in spreading cultural values in the next decades is undeniable, especially in the context of the international market.

Audiovisual productions, and their different display outlets, seem to be the media contents with greatest reach and scope.

Cinema, an industry aimed at entertainment and with also an influence on culture, offers values underlying diversity: production in different languages, with different approaches and world views. The number of films produced has increased, however, they still show the characteristic of a fragmented market.

Regarding the incidence of television, it should be highlighted that currently in 98% of homes in the Europe there is a television set and that the average viewing time is around three hours a day. The massive television audience, which includes all social and cultural strata, and the capacity of different formats for television to integrate cultural values allows for a more inclusive assessment for the purposes of this work. The role of television goes beyond that of a mere transmitter of contents since it contributes to the reinforcement of cultural ties and belonging to a social group.

The emergence of the multimedia communications sector has brought about a new development in audiovisual products and although, for the moment, consumption is not high, they are perceived as the immediate future of communications. At the end of the year 2000, 420 million people were estimated to have access to Internet worldwide, with a quarterly growth of 14.1%. Digital television throws up more decisive data since it is forecast that by the end of 2001, 30 million homes will have access to interactive digital television services and of these, 62% will be European households, as opposed to 18% North-American, 10% from Asia and Oceania and 1% Latin American. As a consequence, the new technologies will be an essential factor for achieving competitive audiovisual products in the global market whilst, at the same time, offering a host of possibilities for production, distribution and conservation of the cultural heritage.

The production and distribution of audiovisual contents which reflect cultural diversity poses significant challenges in a globalized world. A concept of cultural diversity is required in order to guarantee:

— More contents in the media which give a fair representation of the cultural variety;

— The harmonization of the needs of communication companies with public interest; the distribution of contents in the media in all the languages spoken by the social groups;

— The development of news and fiction products by authors who belong to cultural minorities;

— Access from any place to the cultural contents desired.

— Countries with a low audiovisual production capacity.

— Small geographical and linguistic areas.

— Defence of multilinguism (dubbing, subtitling and multilingual production). These elements are of help for knowing the diversity of the audiovisual industry, but are insufficient for distinguishing in what measure a programme defends cultural values or not.

— The preservation of the cultural diversity, among other things, promoting the production and distribution of quality audiovisual contents which reflect the different cultural and linguistic identities". Therefore, in those audiovisual contents we can determine whether a product is dominated by its own cultural values or by alien ones. From here arises the need to establish some precise criteria of measurement for the contents, and not only for the productive capacity of a country.

— "National identity", determined by the nationality of the production company of the programme, the nationality of the main character and the place where the action takes place.

— The language it is broadcast in and the original language of production. In the analysis carried out, these indicators have been complemented by others compiled.

Up till now, general television has maintained its hegemony as a medium of consumption of information and entertainment. However, the progressive increase in the offer, boosted by the appearance of digital platforms, means that in the foreseeable future there will a decrease in audience levels for traditional television. Meanwhile, the current situation suggests that the contents of the general networks, with the object of knowing the type of cultural values they transmit, could be of great interest.

To obtain a more complete picture of the tendencies in programme scheduling and their relationship to cultural diversity, it seems a good idea to complement the high audience programmes with the analysis of specifically cultural programmes in different television stations. The aim is to make a selection from the different productions analysed of those which meet a series of criteria allowing them to be presented as quality programmes. Obviously the idea of quality is prone to subjective assessments and a disparity of professional and technical criteria, for which reason there is no unanimity on criteria. It could be said that there are as many professional perspectives on quality as there are professionals who work in the production of a programme.

In the case of cultural spaces, there is a greater difficulty to achieve a mass audience that will guarantee its success, because, in many cases, the subjects hold little attraction, they have low budgets, limited resources and are broadcast in marginal timetables.

The quality of a television programme can be examined from two fundamental perspectives: technical excellence and content. In his analysis of British programmes, Nossiter finds a certain consensus on three requirements for a programme to be considered of quality: clarity of aim, innovation and relevance. Legatt formulates ten basic criteria which define the parameters for quality according to the contributions of numerous professionals, mainly producers of information programmes. In accordance with these criteria, the following parameters for quality in a cultural programme were established:

a) Formal elements

— *Production level:* good use of available resources.

— *Production:* the programme has a good aesthetic look, with a good image.

— *Presenter's communicating capacity:* he or she manages to connect with the audience.

b) Content elements

— *Innovative treatment:* the resources of the television medium are used to get the most out of the contents.

— *An attractive approach:* there is a clear aim and motivation in the way of tackling certain subjects.

— *Well constructed narrative:* a good pace is kept up which is appropriate for the issues presented.

— *Contact with the TV viewer:* the audience is involved in some way.

Relevance of subjects touched upon: important subjects are tackled and their implications are shown, seeking to widen the viewer's cultural horizons.

Prestige: It becomes a programme of reference for a sector of the audience Machet and Robillard have systemised the criteria adopted by several institutions for the assessment of the production of cultural programmes.

The idea of the public service of broadcasting is argued from a perspective of cultural policy, since it is considered as a medium to ensure the so called "external benefits", that is, to cover certain collective needs of a democratic society. Heilbrun and Gray sum up the external benefits of cultural products which could also be applied to quality cultural programmes:

— They constitute a legacy for future generations (cultural heritage).

— They promote local and national identity and prestige directed towards the exterior.

— Availability: certain cultural products must be available for the public.

— They contribute to the liberal education of the public, and to participation in the arts.

— They promote artistic innovation which, at the same time, adds to the cultural heritage.

Meida and Judicial Betterment

Today the world is a changed place, due in part to advances in mass communications. We see humanitarian crises as they unfold. We get to judge for ourselves the truthfulness of leaders questioned by journalists before the cameras. The net result is that governments have been forced to be more open and accountable. Governments now must take into account public opinion in ways they never had to before. Gone are the days when powerful rulers could operate largely in secrecy, indifferent to their citizens' views.

As people everywhere have grown accustomed to being better informed about developments in their nation and around the world, a byproduct has been to endow the messengers with recognition and consequently great influence. For better or for worse, the media have considerable power to influence people favorably or unfavorably toward those in government.

It comes as no surprise that the courts, the judiciary, and the legal profession have not escaped heightened media scrutiny. Today, the media capitalize on an enduring American appetite for the law and regularly turn to it both to provide information and to captivate. More and more time in the nightly newscasts and space in the daily newspaper are devoted to judicial proceedings, especially criminal cases. Stories with legal themes are also a staple of book publishers, moviemakers, and television drama producers in the U.S. Indeed, much of the fictionalized material is simply repackaged news stories.

American interest in the application of law to life in the United States is rooted in the nation's origins. The Founding Fathers had one thing in common - a deep distrust of the potential for the abuse of power by rulers. Therefore, the Constitution was written to ensure the United States would be governed by the rule of law and not a system based on anyone's societal status.

These concepts of equal application of the law, fundamental fairness, and due process were embedded in the American consciousness from the beginning of the Republic, which is why the themes of right and wrong and fair play appear regularly in U.S. media entertainment and news coverage. These are values that Americans have come to care about passionately - ones that are regularly monitored as they observe their courts in action.

At the same time, another critical factor in the increasing and intense public focus on U.S. courts and the cases filed in them is simply human nature. Whether told in the daily news or fictional story telling, Americans are curious about what happens to others. People are interested in people - the hardships they face, the way they wrestle with challenges, and their exultations in triumph over adversity.

Nowhere is there a greater source for compelling stories than in those cases filed every day in U.S. courts. Now that the courts have come under the media's microscope, they likely will remain there. The heightened demand for information from the courts has required significant changes in the way the courts have traditionally operated. As with most changes, there have been both positive and negative consequences.

A positive byproduct of the changes spurred by the media and addressed by the courts is that more Americans are aware of their constitutional rights than ever before. They are more familiar with how police investigate crime and how the courts try the case to determine guilt or innocence. In short, citizens are more aware of the law and its impact on them than their forefathers were.

On the other hand, the new demands of the media can create internal conflict for judges as they attempt to reconcile two obligations seemingly at odds with each other. For example, ethical rules governing U.S. judges require them to refrain from public comment about a case before the court. The prohibition against such commentary is designed to make sure the judge does not say anything that might cause the public to question his or her impartiality.

Most media questions a judge will face, however, will deal with a specific pending case because it is newsworthy at the moment. Consequently, judges have to become more media savvy. They have to find ways to assist reporters in getting the story while at the same time staying within the boundaries of ethical rules about public comment. Since the courts have no enforcement powers in and of themselves, U.S. judges know that their authority exists only to the degree that the people have confidence in the courts' integrity and fairness in administering justice. Because most people do not attend court regularly, perceptions of the quality of justice come largely from media accounts of the courts' work. That means more courts now try to cooperate more fully with the media to help educate the public about the judicial system.

The media share the courts' recognition that improved cooperation is necessary to strengthen the public's confidence in both institutions. A 2002 survey commissioned by the American Bar Association found that lawyers, judges, and the media need to do a better job in earning the public's trust.

According to the survey, only 19 percent of U.S. citizens say they are "extremely or very confident in" lawyers and the legal profession. The judiciary rated higher at 33 percent, and the media came in lower at 16 percent. By comparison, the medical profession led the list of possibilities at 50 percent.

One of the positive ways the media have affected the judicial system is to help spur a greater sense of openness by the courts so the public can see for itself how the court serves the people. At the same time, the media have begun to focus on the activities of individual judges as well, sometimes to the judge's detriment. For example, a Denver, Colorado, television station followed the state's judges to their annual three-day judicial education workshop. The required workshop was designed to keep judges current with changes in the law and was funded with money from the state. The TV station used hidden cameras to show that nine out of the 300 judges enrolled in the workshop engaged in recreational activities instead of attending some of the classes. The judges caught on camera were certainly embarrassed when it looked like they were vacationing at taxpayers' expense, exemplifying how expanded media coverage can have a negative effect on the image of the courts.

However, the media would argue that exposing public

officials who are not performing their required duties is a positive public service. Whatever one's point of view, the fact remains that the media's increased focus on the courts also includes focusing more intensely on the individual judges themselves.

The area where increased media coverage has caused U.S. courts the greatest concern is the pretrial news coverage in a criminal case. The difficulty is that the U.S. Constitution sometimes pits the courts and media against each other in a clash of amendments. The First Amendment guarantees the media freedom to report just about anything it wants to, including as many details as the media can learn about the arrest of a criminal suspect. The Sixth Amendment guarantees a defendant a fair and public trial, with the burden of ensuring fairness implicitly placed on the trial judge.

Because the U.S. uses a jury system, ordinary citizens of the community determine the guilt or innocence of a defendant. The problem arises when potential jurors learn from the media facts or purported facts about the case that are not permitted to be introduced at trial. An example might be when the police announce to the media that the defendant has confessed to the crime.

However, at a later hearing the judge might rule that the confession was unlawfully obtained by police and will not permit the prosecutor to introduce the confession as evidence. In effect, the judge has to hope that the jurors selected to hear the case will have the ability to disregard knowledge of the confession they read about in the newspaper or heard on television. If the jury cannot disregard that evidence, the trial no longer is considered fair.

When media coverage of a trial is especially heavy, the courts often have to consider alternative and more expensive means of guaranteeing a fair trial. These alternatives include:

— Transferring the entire trial to another city where the news coverage has not been as strong;

— Directing the jury not to read newspapers or watch TV newscasts;

— Issuing "gag orders" that direct the prosecutor, defense attorney, and other court personnel not to talk to the media about the case; or,

— In rare cases, keeping the jury sequestered in a hotel where they are monitored and prevented from accessing the media.

"High profile" cases, such as the O.J. Simpson murder trial in 1995, draw extreme media coverage and have caused significant problems for the courts. In addition to the routine coverage of the trial, the courts now have to contend with evening television talk shows where attorneys talk about what happened in the trial that day and speculate on what will transpire in future days. The result is that the serious trial can begin to seem like a spectacle, much as sports contests fuel talk shows that second-guess and analyze the game. Judges now have reason to worry about the public perception of the courts when individual cases are treated similarly to sporting events.

Judges are also concerned about the potential for erosion in the public's confidence, because there have been a few cases in U.S. history where media coverage appears to have affected the fundamental fairness of the trial. For instance, the 1935 trial of Richard Bruno Hauptmann, accused of kidnapping and murdering the son of aviator Charles Lindbergh, drew unprecedented media coverage. Hauptmann was convicted, but subsequent research has raised questions as to whether the media frenzy created a rush to judgment that caused an innocent man to be convicted.

The media coverage in the 1954 case of Dr. Sam Sheppard

was so pervasive that the U.S. Supreme Court used that case to place the responsibility on the trial court judge to prevent prejudicial publicity. Dr. Sheppard was charged with the murder of his wife and his story was the basis for the American television series (and later film) "The Fugitive."

It is fear of the possibility of media coverage adversely affecting the quality of justice that leads the U.S. Supreme Court to prohibit television coverage of its arguments. The Court has permitted audio taping, but, until recently, has only released the tapes for historical or archival purposes long after the cases were decided.

The recent case involving the 2000 presidential election between then-Governor George W. Bush and former Vice President Al Gore was the first instance of the Court releasing the audiotape in a timely fashion for the news media to cover the event. Whether that will lead to further relaxation of electronic media coverage of the Court remains to be seen.

A related problem is the question of public access to the trial itself. Increasingly, television stations are asking courts to permit "live" coverage of trials. They argue that the public has a right to see the trial and that limited seating in the actual courtroom should not be a bar to the public because TV cameras can bring the trial to the public in their homes.

Opponents, however, argue that the presence of television cameras will change the behavior of the witnesses and court personnel in ways that will affect the fairness of the trial. At present, no TV cameras are permitted in U.S. federal courts. Each state is permitted to decide for itself whether to accept televised trial coverage, and the issue of televised proceedings is one on which the courts have not yet reached consensus.

The first television coverage of a court case is believed to have taken place in Oklahoma City, Oklahoma, in 1953 in the criminal trial of Billy Eugene Manley. The first "live" broadcast of a trial occurred in 1955 when Harry L. Washburn was tried for murder in Waco, Texas. In 1984, CNN broadcast the first nationally televised "live" coverage of a trial in New Bedford, Massachusetts, where multiple defendants were accused of raping a woman on a barroom pool table at a local bar. The strong interest in that case led to the creation of Court TV, which offers daily coverage of court activities, focusing on America's most newsworthy and controversial legal proceedings in courtrooms where live coverage is permitted.

Currently, 25 states permit televised coverage when the presiding judge agrees to let the cameras into the courtrooms. Eight states restrict televised coverage when witnesses object to having television cameras in the courtroom. And 17 states essentially prohibit TV coverage at the trial level through a variety of court rules. There are, however, indications that more courts are opening their doors to the media.

What judges have discovered in the wake of expanded news media coverage is that the old ways and traditional personnel will not be sufficient to cope with modern demands. That is why more courts are hiring specialists, called court public information officers, to work with the media. These media liaisons serve three purposes:

— They are a resource for reporters to check their facts and help ensure accurate reporting of the court's work;

— They provide a court spokesperson who can answer media questions, thus protecting the judge from inadvertently making a comment to the press that violates ethical rules; and

— They provide the court with a specialist who knows how to promote the good news of the courts' work to the media in a newsworthy manner.

Additionally, more U.S. courts are providing information directly to the public through their own web sites on the Internet. The advantage the courts see in this change is that it allows greater control over what information is provided to the public. It also provides the public -- including the media – with electronic access, which reduces the amount of time court personnel spend searching paper files for reporters. Finally, it provides the court with an alternative means of correcting the record when the court feels the media have inaccurately reported on a case.

Just as other segments of society today have had to adjust to advancing technology and expanded communications, so too have U.S. courts. But one thing remains certain. While the courts and media have made adjustments in how they operate in this changing environment, both have remained true to their vital roles in the American democratic system. The late, great CBS newsman Edward R. Murrow captured the importance of courts and media to the United States when he said, "What truly distinguishes a free society from all others is an independent judiciary and a free press."

However the day-to-day interaction between the courts and media may be altered in the future, both will make the changes with an eye always on their mission of safeguarding the freedoms of the citizens they serve.

Media's Role in Women's Progress

Power is the ability to move something in a direction you want- a physical object or an objective you wish to attain. The more people working with you, the more power you have and the better and faster you can move your object or objective. The more people you can reach with your information, the larger the number who will find your goal is also their goal and join with you in attaining it. Thus, having a means of reaching people is crucial to increasing your power.

Owners of mass media reach millions frequently; women's media reach thousands infrequently. Thus, power (the ability to move things your way) depends on the number of people you can reach with your information. The source of power (where you obtain it) is media (i.e., having a means of communication). More people we reach, the more power we have.

Progress is doing better today than yesterday in the pursuit of your interests or use of your abilities. The more options one has, in political, economic, social, and personal areas of life-without social or economic penalties-the more will be taken up and the greater the resulting progress-the larger the number making better use of their abilities, the greater the benefit to society and to other women, as well as to the individuals taking up the options. The key to the progress, therefore, is having means to communicate option.

The owners of mass media select and repeat, to the millions they reach, all options they think are important for people to know about. If others are to be offered, they will have to come from elsewhere, primarily from women themselves, communicated through whatever media they own or are able to use. Thus the key to women's progress is having media to communicate as wide a choice as they know.

Women had virtually no media of their own during the 1950s. Research is needed on the extent of women-owned media in this period. Male-owned media offered and repeated one role, based on a psychological theory that women were by nature subordinate to men and labeled "unnatural" roles other than housewife and mother. Research needed on extent this role was heard in 1950s compared to number of people hearing contradictory evidence.

As the 50s and 60s proceed, fewer and fewer women

entered, or advanced in, other roles. Research: This correlation needs study and documentation, especially by occupation. Some women believed the psychological theory, seeing confirmation in their own experience, and others, hearing no dissent and thinking that media mirrored society, concluded they were alone in not believing the theory and did not try to communicate with other women. Some were eventually persuaded against their own first hand information because the repetition of the theory from a wide variety of sources created the impression of confirmation of it.

Communication began when, for growing numbers of women, their first hand information accumulated sufficiently, showing the inferiority/superiority psychological theory to be false. This caused anger, the natural response to discovering you were lied to, and aroused women to correct the lies, thus causing communication by creating media to communicate their new and corrective information in these ways:

1) *person-to-person contact*, wherever they met-conferences, meetings, consciousness-raising groups;
2) *starting women's media*: journals, newspapers, magazines, making tapes and films, writing books and songs;
3) getting their information into mass media.

This communication then caused action, by women who saw new roles in this new information and took up some of those options. This caused progress, resulting from talents better used and providing new role models for still more women, and leading to expansion of the movement for women's progress. Extension of the progress to all women requires as a first step protecting the existence of women-controlled media to prevent a return to the 1950s, and secondly, to expand all forms of communication for women's information-in mass media, women's media and more person-to-person meetings.

Study is encouraged, for any country and any period, of the extent of the correlation between women's having a means of communication and making progress. For example, consideration may be made of these four major times that women had media of communication for their information:

— *Abolition Movement*: Women working in the church abolition societies obtained media when welcomed into the men's abolition movement and encouraged to write for the abolition press and speak on the lecture platform.They used these media to convey information not only on abolition, one of the women's issues, but on other women's issues, such as women's rights. rogress resulted as new options were offered to women: writing, editing, publishing newspapers, public speaking, political activity, organization, conventions, etc. Seeing this, men withdrew their media from use by women to communicate these options and described the women in terms which inhibited others from associating with them; men could reach more people with their information than the women could reach to correct it.

— *Progressive Movement/World War I*: Women, particularly active in the reform movements of the late 1800s were given media for reform articles, for example in the "muckraking" period of early 1900s when mass magazines were devoted to exposes to obtain certain reform legislation. This made their names known and created an audience for whatever they wrote. Now able to reach the public, women used the media to provide information on their issues of peace and women's rights, as well as humanitarian, economic and political reforms. But before men could take back the media they had provided, World War I was on and they extended their media further to encourage women to take up new options outside the home in new fields of employment replacing men going to war. Women used their access to the public through these media for a concentrated drive for suffrage. The resulting progress, after so extended a period of being able to reach so many of the public, was the 19th Amendment granting the right to vote to women and wide dissemination of the option of political activity, including running for office, which a great many women did in 1920 and the next few years.

Male-owned media were withdrawn for this information in the 1920s; women activists were described as radicals, and a new psychological theory was popularized portraying women as sex objects. Unable to communicate their own information, including the information that many women were exercising their new political rights, especially running for office, women's political activity began to diminish for lack of support. Fewer heard the options and still fewer took them up. Most women, and most people, heard only that these women were "radicals" but no information from the women themselves.

— *World War II:* Media were extended to women to recruit out of the home into war employment in a variety of new fields. Women used the media again to talk about women's issues, new options for women in economic, political and social life, calling for 50% women at peace table, etc. A new women's movement began to arise. Women kept their own names after marriage, a new high number did not marry, as some women took up the new options in personal and professional life offered.

Between 1946 and 1947, media dropped its coverage of women abruptly and increased its domestic and parental articles and news coverage of women as belonging in the home. Family size increased, women dropped out of public life, fewer entered new fields, and employed women made no further advances.

— *The Present:* Women established their own media and obtained mass media coverage of some of their information by demonstrations, sit-ins, legal actions. Women used these media to tell their stories about women's experience and analyze the politics of sexism. They gave new information about discrimination against them; about health, abortion, child care possibilities; about new occupations and new lifestyles, personal and political, not previously offered. As some women avail themselves of new options, progress is being made in some areas.

Mass media are trying to withdraw their media as a means of conveying women's programming or articles conveying women's rights information, and they have begun to describe women as extremists, "aggressive," or "bra-burners," showing them to be as violent as men and as criminally inclined, or always fighting among themselves whenever they get together, or dedicated to destroying the family, or portraying them as sex objects suitable for attack by men out on the street.

Mass Media as a Means of Governance

The free press right of the individual was lost when individuals could no longer afford to exercise it to reach any significant percentage of the population. The press of 1789, when the First Amendment was written, was basically the same as the Gutenberg press of 1450, capable of printing some 300 newspapers per day. Nearly anyone could have a press in those days and reach the same number of people as anyone else. In this context, the First Amendment's freedom of the press was written as a protection for individuals - like the other four First Amendment freedoms, speech, religion, petition, and assembly, which were also to protect the rights of individuals , regardless of the size of their pocketbooks.

By the 1830's, newly invented high-speed presses made the independent printer an employee of the rich person who could afford the very high cost of the new presses, which now printed thousands of copies per day and reached thousands of people that the rest of the public could not reach. Even elected officials could no longer reach their constituents without going through a third party. Mass media - and unequal power - began in the 1830's.

The U.S. population continued to grow and so did the cost of ever-larger presses to reach it, eventually forcing out even rich individuals in favor of corporations. To finance today's media - the extensive media chains, TV networks, and satellites - new combinations have been formed, made up of conglomerates, multinational corporations, and governments.

Corporations, whose major stockholders are often other corporations, usually banks, assert that the Constitutional free press right applies to them. Not only are these corporations not themselves individuals, they prevent individuals from communicating by exercising a monopoly on the means of communication to large numbers and not letting individuals use that media for the information they wish to convey to the public.

Rather than being a "free press" media as envisaged by the writers of the First Amendment, these corporations are essentially distributors of a commodity, namely, information, the same as any business which harvests, collects, and manufactures goods for distribution. They hire employees who will do the gathering and distributing in a businesslike way, safeguarding the economic and political interests of their employers.

Research is also needed of the distribution structure of each major media form: film, art, music, video, cable, newspapers, television, radio, magazines, book publishing, bookstores, satellite communications and other media and major distributors of these media, examining the number of owners, gender, cost of entry, number and percentage of people reached by each, and proportion of mass and other media to total number of people to determine the extent to which the media serve as expression for very few and extent the few are male.

Those who control the means of communication could in every period from the earliest times decide what information people had (about things outside their knowledge from first hand experience), upon which they based their judgments. Before the invention of printing, organized religions were the mass media (by reaching nearly everyone). When the Church said Holy Wars were necessary, they took place, just as happens with today's mass media (which reach nearly everyone). As then, we come to its conclusions because nearly all of us have only its information.

All of history needs to be reexamined, looking at mass media not as simply supplying an account of what happened but as a cause of events by providing information on which people made their decisions. Ask: What information did the majority of people have? Cause can be determined analytically: if 80% of the public had AA information, 2% had BB information, and 18-20% had no information on the subject, the decision made would be a logical decision on AA information. It is necessary to locate the source of information in order to determine selection, repetition, and circulation figures, but it is not necessary to make a value judgment on the media owners' motives, since all media owners have a right to select, repeat, and circulate to as many as they can, information they think is important for others to have, reflecting their class and sex and acting, necessarily, in their own self-interest. Value judgments may be left to the recipients of the information we research. To the extent we can find such data, this informational basis for the reexamination of history will provide us actual, logical, and factual causes of events, past and present.

The following are a few historical periods in which such a reexamination might be made on this informational basis:

— Mass media distribution in the millions, free or very cheap, of copies of tracts and sermons and Horatio Alger-type novels in the later 1800s expounding the "Social Darwinism" theory that (among other things) possession of great wealth was proof of natural superiority and that "survival of the fittest" also applied to ideas : if an idea is heard everywhere and is generally accepted, that proves it is superior to ideas with less circulation, less well believed, and that then do not "survive." Determine circulation figures, before any public choice has had a chance to evidence itself, as first print run on books, advertising circulation figures, retail display space given in advance of any public response to a new book, magazine, record, film, etc.

— What information did people have and from what sources, about Frances Wright in the late 1820's when the public was hearing and considering the ideas of the nation's first women's movement and when the working public changed from supporting to opposing the Workingmen's Parties, the nation's first national effort to broaden its democratic base and significantly to expand the exercise of its free press right.

— Circulation figures for information about public support for "The Great Upheaval" of railroad strikes before and after the meeting in 1877 of the Western Associated Press and cooperating media, which yielded the "Compromise of 1877."

— Circulation figures and sources for information about alternative roles for women (economic, political, social), women's issues (such as childcare centers), and women's ideas and opinions before, during, and after World War I and

World War II.

— Circulation figures for information that women's movement ideas were "communistic" during the "Red Decade" of the 1920s and the "McCarthyism" period after World War II. Include and compare sources and circulation of that information not only in mass media but also in the labor press, women's press, the "left" or "liberal" press.

— Trace circulation figures and sources for information about Freud's concepts of women, from the first mention of Freud in scholarly or in popular press through peaks of promotion of "popular psychology" in 1920s and 1950s. Also trace circulation figures for "popular psychology" ideas that deal with women not specifically attributed to Freud.

— Information supplied the public, including the three branches of government, upon which decisions were and are made by them to support mass media corporate entities over the efforts of individuals to exercise their rights to a free press. For example, studies could be made of circulation figures for information supporting SBA (Small Business Administration) policy of refusing to make loans to small media on the grounds it would interfere with freedom of the press; supporting broadcast licensees' sole right to decide news information content on public airwaves, subject only to expensive legal challenge; supporting Constitutional copy right protection in a way that favors corporate media over individuals; and supporting other legislative, administrative, and judicial decisions that reinforce corporate media as having press rights superior to individual rights in information gathering.

— Similar studies could be made of the circulation figures for information (1) that mass media corporations are a "public institution" or "public utility"; (2) that these corporations have a "duty" to report other people's news (compare this with circulation figures for information describing the origin (in what legislation or by what other public mandate) of this media "obligation" or "right; (3) that they should or can determine what the public has a "right to know" (trace origin, source and circulation figures for the "right to know" expression); (4) that private corporations in the business of distributing information for profit thereby assume these rights over and superior to the individuals' rights to privacy or to disseminate their own information; (5) that mass media are our "free press" but, at the same time, that no individual or group has a right to print or say anything they want to in the mass media. Compare circulation figures for information which the public has that applauds, or justifies, the nation's present media structure with circulation figures for information the public hears that is critical or that suggests changes.

The protest movements of the 1960s and 1970s were-and are-an attempt by various segments of the American public to reach other Americans with their information, information that had or has not been taken into account by the public in making national policies, because it was not heard. The variety of methods used in the protest movement represent efforts to find new ways to reach the public with information considered important for the public to have. The protest movements can be studied as parts of a single movement to expand the nation's communications system to include more information from a larger number of the American public.

Examination is needed in depth, documented and statistically measured, of methods used by the owners of mass media to resist the movement of people who feel that the existing media do not communicate their information to the public and are trying to persuade media to expand their information coverage. Consider, for example, these media ways of responding: By not reporting the informational aspects of the movement. By repeating frequently the assertion that groups of the public are trying to "use" the media, implying they should not try to communicate directly to the public. By describing criticism of mass media as an attack on freedom of the press. By characterizing the protest movement as "disruptive of democracy and orderly government" and/or characterizing them as "a tiny minority of extremists," thus discouraging the public from listening to the protesters' information even when they receive it.

Media's Role in Revealing Corruption

Freedom of the press, including free access to information, is fundamental to open, democratic society. This view has found its way into international legal norms and, in numerous countries, the media's rights are upheld and guaranteed in freedom of information legislation. In spite of the international recognition of press freedom, journalists and media organisations throughout the world continue to face obstacles in reporting. Obstruction is reflected in the presence of active censorship or restrictive regulations on journalistic work, limited or blocked access to official information, legal landscape that inhibits the ability of journalists to inquire and report freely such as the application of draconian defamation and sedition laws – and a censorious abuse of essential media services, such as broadcasting, printing facilities and distribution systems. In addition, the lack of training, poor professional standards and a dearth of investment into investigative reporting make it difficult and sometimes impossible for journalists to access, impart or disseminate accurate information.

A difficult relationship between journalism and political power is a hallmark democratic society. To that extent, a tendency to manipulate news and shape the agenda of public debate exists in all societies. In countries where democratic culture is not well established, restrictions on media tend to be more explicit and profoundly damaging to debate or public engagement. Where the affairs of government or powerful interest groups are protected by secrecy, journalists face considerable obstacles – and physical risk – if they embark upon investigations that could lead exposing corruption. Yet the media also face challenges within their own ranks.

Civil society has been monitoring developments in ownership concentration, the role of advertising and corrupt journalistic practices that undermine the media's ability to adhere to internationally accepted standards. Since the events of September 11th, new measures to block, reduce or slow down the flow of information – while increasing surveillance of access itself – have threatened to restrict media freedom. In Jordan, for instance, new amendments to the penal code subject journalists to prison terms for publishing material that 'could breach national unity, divide the population or damage the image and reputation of the state'. In Saudi Arabia, all Internet service providers must now keep records of their users in order to track access to forbidden websites.

The United States has begun withholding information deemed detrimental to 'institutional, commercial, and personal privacy interests'. Increased surveillance of the Internet, e-mail and telephone conversations was authorised in both Britain and Canada, while new French laws effectively criminalise the encryption of electronic messages. In Germany, a new anti-terrorist law grants intelligence services the right to access stored telecommunications data and trace the origins of e-mail.

Simply by doing their jobs well, independent-minded journalists have played a central role in promoting democracy for many years. Many put their lives or freedom at risk to promote transparent and accountable governance and corporate behaviour. Of the 68 confirmed cases of murders of journalists in 2001, 15 were Access to information related to their investigative work on issues of corruption. This is an alarmingly high number. One victim was Parmenio Medina Pérez, producer at Costa Rica's Radio Monumental. On 7 July 2001, he was shot three times by unknown assailants just outside his house; he died upon arrival at hospital. Pérez had produced a weekly satirical radio programme called *La Patada* (The Kick), known for a hard-hitting approach to official corruption. One report accused a local Catholic radio station and its director, Minor de Jesús Calvo Aguilar, of fiscal improprieties. The Catholic Church subsequently closed the station and fraud investigators started examining Aguilar's finances. Pérez began to receive death threats shortly thereafter. In the meantime, a judge ruled in favour of Aguilar and ordered the station back on air. In another case, Georgy Sanaya, a popular Georgian journalist, was found dead in his Tbilisi apartment on 26 July 2001. He had been shot in the head at close range. Sanaya had anchored *Night Courier*, a nightly political talk show on independent television station Rustavi-2 on which he interviewed Georgia's leading politicians. Rustavi-2's executive director claimed that the murder was probably intended to intimidate the station, which is known for its investigative reporting on the abuse of power.

Although Sanaya did not receive any personal threats, the station was frequently the target of government harassment. The police arrested a suspect in August 2001, but released him for lack of evidence. One of the most significant results of Sanaya's murder case has been a heightened public awareness of the threat to Georgia's independent media. This case and others prompted major public demonstrations against government interference in the media, inducing President Eduard Shevardnadze to dismiss his entire cabinet in early 2002. Killings continue. Edgar Damalerio, managing editor of the Filipino weekly newspaper *Zamboanga Scribe*, was shot dead on 13 May 2002. His colleagues are convinced that Damalerio, known for his critiques of corruption among local politicians and the police, was killed for his journalistic work. Valery Ivanov, editor of the newspaper *Tolyatinskoye Obozreniye* in Togliatti in south Russia, was killed on 29 April 2002. The newspaper was well known for its reports on organised crime and official corruption.

In Bangladesh, Harunur Rashid, a reporter for the daily newspaper *Dainik Purbanchal*, was killed after writing several stories on official corruption and links between criminal syndicates and outlawed Maoist guerrilla groups. Orlando Sierra Hernández, a columnist for the Colombian newspaper *La Patria*, was shot in the head on 30 January 2002, and died two days later. His columns frequently attacked government corruption and human rights abuses by left-wing guerrillas.

Apart from direct physical threats against journalists, the media in many countries face legislation that prevents them from gaining access to and imparting informa-tion. Repressive defamation laws that put the burden of proof on journalists and grant special protection to public officials exist across Eastern Europe, Africa, Asia and parts of Latin America.

These laws often forbid truth as a defence in defamation cases, signalling that the reputation of public officials is deemed worthier of protection than the public's right to know. Such laws – and the concomitant threat of prison sentences – create a climate of fear that discourages investigative reporting and the exposure of corruption. One example of severely repressive legislation is Kazakhstan's libel law, which is used to financially weaken media critical of the political and commercial oligarchy. Almaty's independent weekly *Nachnem s Ponedelnika* is known for its in-depth reporting on state officials' involvement in the oil trade and other contracts. From 1998 to 2001, the weekly was sued 17 times for defamation, chiefly by officials or company executives with close links to government. In three cases, the paper was found guilty of slander and fined a total of 25,935,000 tenge (about US $180,000). Since Kazakh libel law does not recognise truth as a defence, *Nachnem s Ponedelnika* was fined for harming the reputation of public officials, without due consideration of possible evidence of their involvement in bribery. Two plaintiffs subsequently dropped their suits but the 12 remaining cases are still pending in the courts. The sheer volume of cases filed suggests systematic harassment of the weekly and the abuse of privacy laws by some state officials.

A recent World Bank analysis of media ownership structures in 97 countries found that state-owned media tend to be less effective than private media in monitoring government. 'Countries that have reduced government ownership of the media have often experienced rapid improvements in the amount and quality of coverage. For example, Mexico's partial privatisation of broadcasting in 1989 led to a sharp increase in coverage of government corruption scandals.'

Compared to other regions, Latin America and the Caribbean have low levels of state ownership of the media, yet both television and the press are concentrated in the hands of only a few private owners. This highly concentrated private ownership, combined with the restrictive regulations found in many Latin American countries, tends to restrain the media.

No analytical reports have identified corrupt practices in media giants. In some cases, however, private media owners themselves can have a strong influence on whether corruption is covered, especially if they pursue greater profits rather than principles of free reporting or access to information. One such example revolves around a major deal struck in September 2001 between the Chinese government and the media giants AOL Time Warner and Rupert Murdoch's News Corporation.

The deal grants both companies the right to broadcast television programmes in China in exchange for beaming Chinese government-sponsored material into the United States. The arrangement was criticised by press freedom organisations, as was Murdoch's decision to remove the BBC World Service from his network after Beijing complained about BBC coverage of internal politics.

The International Federation of Journalists (IFJ) argued that the landmark deal with China 'sidelines human rights and press freedom' while showing indifference to the plight of journalists and programmers in Chinese jails. The actions of AOL Time Warner and News Corporation sent out a message that promoting access to information – the basis for exposing corruption – was not a priority consideration in their decision-making. Such conflicts of interest fall into sharper relief when media control and political power are combined in a single individual. One of the clearest such embodiments is Italy's prime minister Silvio Berlusconi, who commands large real estate holdings, owns several major newspapers and also controls most of Italy's private television market. As head of the government, he can now control the country's public television market since he effectively nominates the director of Radio Televisione Italiana (RAI). Berlusconi had promised to resolve the conflict between his political role and commercial interests within the first 100 days of his administration. This period has long since expired and at this writing Berlusconi had yet to install an effective firewall between his dual roles of prime minister and media mogul.

RAI and Berlusconi's media enterprises enjoy a certain editorial independence under a collective national agreement. In reality, however, journalists reporting too aggressively on the prime minister's business interests risk inconvenient transfers or the permanent loss of their jobs. Journalists have delivered confidential reports to the national press association concerning newsroom practices that discourage criticism of the government.

In the United States, where media organisations undertake major lobbying efforts to promote their business interests, not all media espouse the role of independent watchdog. Both major parties receive donations from the media, which also sponsor members of Congress who support their objectives. Between 1993 and June 2000, the media provided a total of US $75 million to politicians. It was money well spent. One of the most remarkable – and least publicised – media events in recent years was the decision in 1996 to make a free gift to broadcasters of portions of the digital spectrum developed for digital data transfer, a deal worth an estimated US $70 billion. This exchange of donations and gifts raises critical questions about the nature of the relationship between the media and government and the media's ability to retain independence.

This independence is also compromised by advertising. Although vital to media companies' financial performance, advertising has had an increasingly pernicious impact on editorial departments. Journalists are increasingly expected to produce material to suit sponsors and advertisers, blurring the line between advertising and editorial content. Some media companies increase revenues by passing off advertising as editorial content; others make favourable coverage of an enterprise contingent upon paid advertising. Among many private newspapers in Africa, the relationship between journalism and advertising is more straightforward. Since advertising departments are often understaffed, reporters are expected to solicit advertising while on assignment, earning a share of the fee if successful. 'Not many journalists will admit it directly,' said Gabriel Baglo, former president of Togo's independent press union, 'but what happens is that journalists go to report on a company. Because they ask them to place an ad at the same time, a deal is struck to ensure favourable coverage of the company's performance.' Similarly, a Tanzanian journalist reports: 'The credibility of the news coverage is rightly questioned. This is especially the case in broadcasting: virtually all radio news in private media is sponsored.'

Corruption also exists within the structure of media organisations and in the way journalists carry out their reporting tasks. Many engage in a host of corrupt practices, ranging from 'chequebook journalism' to news tailored to suit advertising or commercial needs. Journalists' codes of conduct condemn such corrupt activities, but the reality of the profession does not mirror its aspirations, especially when underpaid – or unpaid – journalists resort to accepting payment in order to make ends meet. Such situations arise in many developing countries and countries in transition, where pay levels are low. While bribes may be small, they can influence the story the journalist writes or broadcasts.

In a 2001 seminar in Kursk, Russia, local newspaper journalists reported that they had accepted payments from a local businessman to write favourable articles about his ventures and investments. In the developed world, the practice of freebies is well established. Journalists enjoy free air travel from airlines and hospitality at hotels and then write glowing travel articles. In Europe, members of media organisations often expect hotels and meals to be complimentary when they attend press conferences; they may even count on sponsors to provide gifts. Such practices can have a direct effect on media coverage, as came to light in the wake of the Enron scandal. Unethical links between financial journalists and the energy giant resulted in uncritical coverage of the company's activities. Irwin Stelzer, a contributor to the *Weekly Standard* in the United States and the *Sunday Times* of London, who complimented Enron in November 2001 for 'leading the fight for competition', publicly disclosed his association with Enron and that of *Weekly Standard* editor William Kristol. Stelzer never disclosed how much he was paid for his work; Kristol received more than US $100,000 for a consultancy contract for the company. 'I'm a little unhappy to have had an association with people who turned out to be not entirely honourable in other dealings,' Kristol said later.

In an effort to curb such activities, some media groups have begun to hold journalists to ethical standards. Russia's journalism union, for example, distributes press cards only to media houses and journalists that adopt its official code of conduct, which condemns corrupt practices and provides for editorial independence.

To promote openness in society and expose corruption, media owners, publishers, editors and journalists must resist pressures to report what is beneficial to political and private interests. They must also overcome obstacles to free reporting, especially in the absence of effective freedom of information legislation.

Editorial independence – the media's right to take editorial decisions according to conscience and codes of conduct – lies at the heart of promoting independent journalism. Journalists and media freedom groups need to lobby media owners and management, regardless of whether they are private or state-owned, to recognise principles of editorial independence that allow journalists to pursue stories in the public interest, including exposés of corruption.

When financially possible, editors and media owners should invest in improved coverage and stop relying on companies or taxpayers to meet their journalists' travel costs. In many cases, refusing freebies or outright bribes presents additional financial hardship for media whose resources are already limited. These media do not even have the resources to allow journalists the time to engage in the extended research or investigations required for professional coverage. Given these circumstances, the international community cannot pass responsibility for curbing corruption on to journalists and media organisations alone.

Although few programmes to support investigative journalism exist, an important component in confronting corruption, a number of specialist organisations do provide training. The Association of Investigative Journalists, the World Bank and Australia's Centre for Democratic Institutions (CDI) have developed training courses for journalists interested in covering corruption. In March 2002, the CDI ran an election reporting workshop in Papua New Guinea that included modules entitled 'covering corrupt politicians' and 'minding your back'. Another initiative is the Journalists Against Corruption (PFC) programme, which was established in 2000 by Probidad, an NGO in El Salvador that promotes democratisation throughout Latin America.

Probidad operates a monitored e-mail system that facilitates the exchange of articles, opinions, announcements, contacts and resources among Latin American journalists who investigate corruption. Journalists identify themselves to a moderator to establish their credentials, but the system guarantees anonymity to journalists who fear recrimination. Probidad has not yet checked the general impact of its initiative, but more than 600 journalists have signed up to the service.

A similar initiative is a website for African journalists reporting on corruption. Established by the IFJ, with funding from the European Commission, the IFJ-PA website offers free information and links to African journalists reporting on finance and corruption issues. Journalists sign up as members by providing references to the site's moderator. Both the Probidad and IFJ initiatives enable journalists to post articles to other journalists or news organisations if their own editors reject them.

Media have to combat corruption in the public and private sectors and within the media world itself. Where freedom of information legislation is lacking or its implementation ineffectual, legal reform initiatives need to be promoted by NGOs as well as public and private interests. In countries with harsh defamation laws, legal defence funds can be instrumental in assisting journalists and news organisations targeted by punitive libel laws.Within the media, conflict of interest legislation must be advocated to counter the concentration of media ownership and ensure the continuity of multiple sources of information. Journalists' initiatives to establish statutes of editorial independence should also be supported by media owners, governments and donor organisations. Rules on corruption in the media should be adopted by the industry, but journalists must also be paid adequate salaries. A clear distinction must also be established between editorial and advertising departments. Naming and shaming colleagues who take bribes or act as consultants to companies they cover can also go a long way towards reducing corruption.

6

Media and Sustainable Future

Although human societies have confronted major hurdles throughout history, the challenges of our era are unique. Never before has the human family been on the verge of devastating the Earth's biosphere and crippling the ecological foundations for countless generations to come. Never before has the entire human family been required to work together to imagine and consciously build a sustainable future. Where local challenges dominated our awareness in the past, now it is the well-being of the entire planet that commands our attention. This is not a concern for the remote future.

Current trends in population growth, resource depletion and pollution suggest we will reach a critical turning point or "evolutionary inflection" within twenty or thirty years—roughly the decade of the 2020s. If this is a valid assessment, then never before in human history will so many people be called upon to make such sweeping changes in so short a time. What kind of world will the next generation inhabit? If we continue along our present course, children alive today will inhabit a planet with a warming climate that wreaks havoc on food production and produces massive waves of famine; with supplies of cheap petroleum exhausted; with widespread deforestation; with the goodwill of the human family ravaged as nations fight over access to remaining resources; with coastal cities inundated by rising seas; with millions of people migrating to resource-favored regions; with solar radiation penetrating through a weakened ozone layer and threatening the Earth's food chain on land and in the seas; with far less farmland and productive topsoil available to feed an additional 3 billion people; with a drastically reduced number of plant and animal species; and with toxic pollution spread throughout the land, water and air.

In short, unless dramatic changes are made in our manner of producing, consuming and living, we will soon create a world filled with monumental destruction, suffering, conflict and despair. There is no necessity that we go down this path and hit the wall of absolute limits to growth. We have the time and opportunity to design ourselves back into nature with ways of living that are adapted to the unique ecology, culture and resources of each bioregion of the planet.

Our evolutionary intelligence is now being tested. Will the human family struggle forward only to fall back before achieving our full measure of development, the Earth's environment crippled by pollution, its abundant resources squandered, and humanity torn apart by chronic conflict? Or, will humanity consciously move through this time of testing and challenge, work diligently to restore the Earth's biosphere to its former beauty and integrity, and seek reconciliation around a future of mutually assured development? We have reached a decisive turning point in human evolution. A positive future will not arrive automatically—it will emerge only if we respond in creative new ways equal to the challenges before us.

What level of response is appropriate to this challenge? If we see our home burning down, we know we must do more than throw a few cups of tea on the blaze. Analogously, if we are to build a sustainable, compassionate and creative planetary civilization, then it is essential that we respond to our global crisis in ways that are equal or proportional to the challenges we face. At least three dimensions of change are essential:

— *Sustainable Direction*. The Earth cannot sustain ten billion people striving for a high-consumption lifestyle. It is imperative that we develop workable visions of sustainable ways of living that offer the potential for an enhanced quality of life.

— *Sufficient Speed*. We have to respond fast enough to match our swiftly changing situation. Even if we move in the right direction, with human inertia it could easily be "too little and too late."

— *Adequate Scope*. Only broad and deep changes—as great as the shift from the agrarian era to the industrial era—will be adequate. We cannot expect marginal measures to suffice (for example, cars with a slightly improved fuel economy, modest recycling measures, etc.). The changes required are sweeping and far-reaching. Currently, most developed nations are:

1) moving in a counterproductive direction with undifferentiated economic growth;
2) mobilizing themselves at far too slow a speed to respond meaningfully to the rapidly developing global crisis; and
3) making only superficial adjustments in our ways of producing, living and consuming.

It is unrealistic to think we can simply regulate or legislate our way into a sustainable, compassionate and creative future for the Earth. In both the public and private sectors, many bureaucracies are already faltering under the weight of their overwhelming size and complexity. Most citizens have seen the limits of bureaucracy and understand that if creative action is required, it can only come through the conscious and deliberate actions of countless individuals working in cooperation with one another. Bureaucracy cannot save us. To realize the changes now essential will require the voluntary choices and actions of millions--even billions—of persons.

Never before in human history have so many people been called upon to make such sweeping changes in so little time. To act with the speed, cooperation and creativity demanded by our situation will require the respectful actions of free individuals consciously acting in concert with one another. How can millions of persons spread around the world achieve this unprecedented level of species-teamwork to build a sustainable and meaningful future? In a word, through communication! It was our ability to communicate that enabled humans to evolve from awakening hunter-gatherers to the verge of global civilization, and it will be a new level and type of communication that will enable us to build a workable and meaningful future.

At every level—local, regional, national and global—we must start communicating, in earnest, to build an authentic base of shared understanding from &Mac226; which to build our common future.

The human family cannot make the sweeping changes that are required—in consumption patterns, energy and transportation policies, the design of communities, international relations, and much more—without a massive increase in the level and quality of communication. People will resist making changes unless—and until—there exists broad agreement about the nature of change. As a first step, people will need to communicate their despair that we can restore the global ecology, their resentments for broken dreams of material prosperity, and their unwillingness to make sacrifices unless there is greater fairness.

Only after a cathartic process of learning, communication and reconciliation will people be ready to act with the level of energy, creativity and cooperation that our circumstances demand. However, once citizens know what other citizens locally—and around the world—are willing to do, and once they are settled in their own minds as to what constitutes appropriate action, then they and their representatives in government can act with authority.

Media Power

A communications revolution is already sweeping the planet. Within a decade we will see the integration of television, computers, satellites, fiber optics and other technologies into a new system with the potential for instantaneous communication around the planet. Already the raw power of television is staggering. For example, in the U.S. 98% of all homes have a TV set—more than have indoor toilets, stoves or refrigerators. What is more, the average person watches more than four hours per day. Not surprisingly, television provides a majority of people with a majority of their news about the world. Roughly 60% of the world now has access to television and this percentage is growing rapidly.

With the speed of light, television extends our involvement to the entire planet. Because we are a visually-oriented species—"one picture is worth a thousand words," "seeing is believing"—television embodies a common, visual language that makes it the primary source of information and understanding for the human family. Through the eyes of television, we can touch the reality of a starving villager in Africa, we can see the effects of acid rain in Germany, we can feel the despair of ghetto residents in New York city, and we can touch the reality of fighting in the streets of Northern Ireland. Television makes every viewer an active witness—a knowing and feeling participant in what is being shown. By any measure, television has become the "social brain" or "central nervous system" for the human family.

Given the pervasiveness of television, we already possess the tools of local to global communication that can transform our semi-conscious drift towards ecological catastrophe into conscious action in support of a sustainable future. However, these tools are not being used to advance civilization; instead, they are being used primarily to advance consumption. In the U.S. the average person sees at least 25,000 commercials a year on TV. Commercials are far more than a pitch for a particular product; they are also advertisements for the attitudes, values and lifestyles that surround the consumption of that product.

Mass entertainment is being used to capture the attention of a mass audience that is then appealed to by mass advertising to promote mass consumption. The programming that goes with this advertising is consciously constructed to provide a psychological context that is congruent with high-consumption lifestyles. For example, advertisers for fast cars, rich foods and luxurious living will not place their ads in programs that might unsettle potential consumers with issues of poverty, injustice and ecological calamity.

Not surprisingly, programming that describes the need for more ecological modes of living almost never appears on television as it would threaten the legitimacy of the culture of conspicuous consumption. By default, we are left with programming and advertising that is profoundly biased and that selectively portrays and powerfully reinforces a materialistic and consumerist view of life. By programming television to achieve commercial success, the mindset of entire nations is being programmed for ecological failure.

The pervasive commercialization of television programming is distorting and undermining the very foundation of civilization—the view of reality and social identity that we hold in common. The consumerist bias of television is no longer an issue of "good taste"—it is a survival issue because it is literally killing us! By promoting consumerism and simultaneously distracting people from the urgency of the global ecological crisis, contemporary television programming is actively creating a civilizational mindset that promotes the devastation of the biosphere.

Television may be our social window onto the world, but the view it provides is cramped and narrow. Television may be the collective mirror in which we see ourselves, but the reflection it gives is often distorted and unbalanced. Television may be the primary story-telling machine through which we find shared meaning in our lives, but the stories it tells are typically shallow, violent, demeaning and shortsighted. Television may function as the barometer of social feeling through which we judge the mood of our communities, country and world, but the feedback it provides is often superficial, consumerobsessed and devoid of soulful qualities.

To repeat, our evolutionary intelligence as a species is being directly tested by how we use our powerful tools of mass communication. Will future generations look back to this pivotal period in human history and conclude that we failed to use our "social brain"—the multi-media television system—to support our healthy evolution? Or will they conclude that citizens of the Earth rose to this time of challenge by consciously mobilizing our tools of mass communication and fostering a dramatic increase in civilizational awareness, consensus and creative action?

Positive Use

The future of our physical environment will depend directly upon the future we make of our electronic environment. Lester Brown, author of the highly respected 'State of the World reports' puts it plainly: "The communications industry is the only instrument that has the capacity to educate on a scale that is needed and in the time available." A number of changes are needed if we are to harness the immense power of the communications industry to build a sustainable future; among them are the following:

— *Earth Commercials*—To balance the onslaught of aggressively pro-consumerist commercials, we need a corresponding number of "Earth commercials" that awaken a compassionate consciousness and encourage people to consume with an awareness of the planet's ecology and the needs of future generations. These could be produced at a low cost, with a high level of humor and creativity, and have an enormous impact in fostering an ecological consciousness.

— *Viewer Feedback Forums*—Television almost never turns its cameras around to look directly at itself and its profound consumerist bias. Ironically, the last taboo topic on television is television itself and how it is reinforcing a consumerist consciousness that, in turn, threatens the evolutionary potential of our species. We need to use television to create highly public forums with live polling and citizen feedback that hold the mass media accountable for presenting a mature and balanced diet of programming.

— *Ecologically Balanced Programming*—The number and intensity of ecologically relevant programs needs to match the magnitude and severity of the problems we face. We need a new balance in our diet of television programming. Currently, the overwhelming majority of programming is devoted to entertainment. We are entertainment rich and knowledge poor. We are like longdistance runners who prepare for marathon races by eating 95% junk food. We need a far healthier diet of images, ideas and messages that portray the reality of our changing world situation.

— *Positive Views of the Future*—We cannot build a future consciously that we have not first imagined. Currently, we are inundated with negative views of the future showing ecological catastrophes and resource wars producing famine and disease. We desperately need positive views that inspire hope and that provide aligning visions for building a sustainable, compassionate and creative future. We need fresh scenarios of the future that portray what life » could be like for families, neighborhoods, cities and the world if we begin the serious work of designing ourselves into a sustainable future.

— *Ecologically Oriented Entertainment Programming*—Because television teaches continuously about the lifestyles and values that are the norm for society, we need entertainment programming that actively explores more ecological ways of living, working, consuming, relating and thinking. We need entertainment programming that explores the many different ways in which we can adapt to the global ecological challenge with alternative ways of living. The portrayal of everyday life in sustainable societies can surely serve as the creative source for for innumerable comedies, tragedies and dramas.

— *Dialogues on the Future*—Television is on the verge of moving from a one-way information system to a two-way communication system. With interactivity, televised forums could be developed where a diverse array of people can speak publicly on behalf of future generations and make appeals to the current generation to rapidly evolve our cultures, worldview, communication priorities, economic activities, and so on. These forums could include live polling and other modes of feedback that enable the average citizen of the planet to become directly involved in the dialogue.

If communication is the critical ingredient for responding to a deteriorating biosphere, and if we already have all of the tools needed to enable us to communicate our way into a sustainable future, then what is stopping us? Many citizens feel the electronic media are part of the problem rather than part of the solution—they assume television cannot be changed, that it will always be in the business of promoting consumption, and that it will never be used to promote an ecological ethic.

Like the early days of the civil rights movement, the feminist movement and the environmental movement, many persons feel powerless to change "the system." Few people realize the extent to which "they own the public airwaves." In fact, if the public were to come together and hold the television industry accountable for their communication needs, change would be rapid and sweeping. Another impediment to change is psychological inertia—the natural, human resistance to fundamental change. Many people do not want to acknowledge how severe and urgent are the challenges we now face—to do so would bring disruption to lives that already seem impossibly stressed and stretched.

Overall, if we are to build a workable future through our voluntary actions, then we need to go beyond our skeptical view that television is only a consumerist medium. We need to assert that we are more than consumers who want to be entertained—we are also citizens who want to be informed and involved in choosing our pathway into the future.

The next few decades will be a decisive time for humanity and the planet. We face an unprecedented crisis where, faster than we expected, the ecological system upon which human civilization depends is unraveling with devastating consequences.

Our situation is so serious and so urgent that we cannot afford to blame one another. We need to work with compassion to awaken the minds and soften the hearts of people who are strongly attached to perpetuating the status quo in business and government.

To build a sustainable future, we need to cultivate a culture of sustainability—a social and psychological mindset as citizens, communities and nations that reflects a new way of thinking about the Earth and a new valuing of future generations. Once established, innumerable actions will flow naturally from a cultural mindset of sustainability. It is primarily through our "social brain" (the television system and its interconnected computer and satellite networks) that this mindset will be established and cultivated.

How we use our tools of mass communication is not just another issue, it is the basis for understanding and responding to all issues. With mass communication we can achieve the level of mass cooperation needed to adapt our manner of living to the new global realities. Assuming that a problem recognized is a problem half solved, then we can make a giant leap forward in coping with the global ecological crisis by simply placing the communications issue on our collective social agenda. This new way of looking at the media is unfamiliar territory for everyone concerned—citizens, political leaders and media managers.

Regulating Media Revolution

The media is going through a period of revolution. The degree of change, in terms of both technological convergence between media and the globalisation of media markets, is massive and far-reaching, and far from completed. The potential for 'interactive television', especially through broad-band cable technology allowing the combination of conventional and interactive television with computer network and telecommunications facilities, demonstrates the need for a regulatory regime based on new foundations.

If concrete evidence of convergence is needed, Marsden provides it when he refers us to an attempt by Microsoft, Intel and Compaq to set PC-dominated standards for digital television, an event which he describes as 'a watershed in the convergence of computing and telecommunications'.

The nature and degree of the media revolution is such that ad hoc, incremental and often reactive change in light of new circumstances will not be sufficient, yet as Humphreys notes in his study of mass media policy in Western Europe, 'Increasingly, public policies have tended to follow technological and market developments'.

If media regulation is to achieve anything meaningful, what is needed as a matter of urgency is a more fundamental review of the rationales, techniques and consequences relating to media regulation, that can lay a sound foundation for responses to ongoing and future developments.

In Oftel's terms, what is needed is 'a systematic effort to ensure consistency of approach to the regulation of communications networks, whether these are wire or fibre-based or wireless, or broadcast or hybrids of these'. However, the challenges to media regulation do not arise solely out of technological developments.

Changes of corporate structure in the media market have produced, for example, the domination of conventional commercial broadcasting in Italy by Berlusconi and the domination of the British press by two news groups, demonstrating the need for reappraisal of the regulatory regime if pluralism is to be maintained. As Bagdikian summarises the issue, 'If a small number of publishers, all with the same special outlook, dominate the marketplace of public ideas, something vital is lost to an open society'.

The kind of international cross-media empire developed by Murdoch, or the dominance of Canal and Kirch on mainland Europe, poses a further clear threat to pluralism, but cannot properly be addressed either on a sectoral basis or within individual legal jurisdictions. Over-spill of broadcasting, across national borders, presents one obvious practical problem for national regulators concerned, for example, with the control of violent or sexually explicit imagery.

Collins and Murroni refer to this phenomenon, succinctly as 'the erosion of national communications sovereignty through technological change'. While the global nature of the Internet presents a particular set of international problems, the US Supreme Court's recent decision regarding the Communications Decency Act 1996 demonstrates the difficulties of legislating on such matters even in a domestic setting.

The maintenance of plurality within a domestic market also becomes more difficult, if not impossible, when ownership is contained within a series of international media conglomerates which may have little in the way of meaningful national affiliations.

From the perspective of ensuring competition, national efforts to limit the growth of cross-media empires may be undermined by the perceived national economic interest in allowing such conglomerates to grow large if they are to compete effectively on the international arena. To quote Bagdikian again, 'some national governments encourage formation of dominant national firms so that they can better compete in a world-wide race'.

These outcomes of the media revolution appear to demand a root and branch review of regulatory policy and practice, yet to date we have seen only marginal changes. Proposals for a single media or communications regulator appear to be gathering momentum, and international, especially European, organisations play an increasingly significant part in media regulation. However, such developments may in themselves be doomed to failure if inadequate consideration is given to what may be considered the first order question of 'why regulate?', or, more specifically, 'what are the objectives and values that underlie the regulatory endeavour?'.

It is useful to start by focusing on a single recent example which epitomises the nature of the issues raised in the context of the changing television market in Britain. While the arrival of Channel 5, the last new national analogue terrestrial licence to be awarded in Britain, could scarcely be described as revolutionary, the imminent arrival of DTT carries with it rather more hopes, expectations and fears. The supposed benefits of digitalisation, in terms of more channels as a result of digital compression, better quality sound and wide screen picture display are seen as the biggest change to television in Britain since the arrival of, depending on which commentator you listen to, colour pictures or the remote control.

However, commentators agree that the electronic programme guides and conditional access systems (CASs) required for the viewer to receive DTT, form new pinch-points in the commercial television market, with control of these gateways permitting the possibility of domination of the market by one player. BSkyB, is already the virtual monopoly player in British satellite television, and is part of Rupert Murdoch's News Corporation group that controls over 35 per cent of the British national press. This group also looks likely to be first in the field with DTT decoders, and, as the probable key supplier of major programming to DTT (through exclusive control of major sporting events and new films) has the potential to develop rapidly a monopoly power over this new market.

Under the new structure created by the Broadcasting Act 1996, and, the Advanced Television Services Regulations 1996 which implements EC Directive 95/47, the telecommunications regulator, Oftel, has now been given a key role in licensing the decoder systems (CASs) which will be necessary in order to receive DTT, and in establishing guidelines for the CAS sector. Oftel's brief extends also to the more general objective of avoiding the risks of abuse of dominant positions within new markets, and it can be argued that this role will be crucial if widespread benefit is to accrue from the advent of the digital era.

In June 1997, despite acknowledging the qualities of a competing bid from Digital Television Network (DTN), the ITC awarded control of the three commercial multiplexes for DTT to the British Digital Broadcasting (BDB) consortium. However, influenced in part, no doubt by advice from Oftel, the ITC was only prepared to accept the BDB bid if BSkyB were to sell its one-third equity holding to the other consortium members, Granada and Carlton.

The losing bidder for the multiplexes, DTN, was reported as considering an application for judicial review in relation to the licence award, however, precedent suggests that such a step would be more related to publicity than anything else, given the courts' track-record of reluctance in overturning ITC licence allocation decisions.

Evidence in this field suggests that the British courts cannot necessarily be relied upon to ensure rationality or even transparency in the exercise of the power such as the award of licences to broadcasters. It can be argued that British courts, basing their actions to a large extent upon the limited concept of 'Wednesbury reasonableness', do not apply the same, rigorous standards of review as do, for example, their US counterparts.

Despite BSkyB's withdrawal from the consortium, Oftel continued to express concern regarding BSkyB's likely position of dominance in relation to programme supply to the new channels, especially in the key areas of sport coverage and movie premieres. Don Cruickshank, Oftel's Director General, noted that, even with BSkyB excluded from holding a share in multiplex licences, 'the participation of BSkyB . . . as a long term supplier of certain pay TV services, in particular sports programming, raised substantial competition concerns in the pay TV network and conditional access markets'. This reflects the situation described by Herman and McChesney in the US, where they note that even organisations of the size of NBC and CBS can be 'shut out' of the system if media giants like Disney and Time Warner increasingly provide their own products, notably films, on a privileged basis to their own channels.

The reactive and marginal reform of the British media regulation regime brought about in recent years has failed to resolve tensions between competing regulatory approaches and philosophies. Indeed, in confirming attempts to allow the co-existence of competing and potentially conflicting rationales, it indicates a degree of complacency and myopia which is likely to prove dangerous in the context of the ongoing media revolution.

A degree of tension between regulators sharing jurisdiction is inevitable, and perhaps even helpful in the short term if it facilitates the articulation of clear regulatory standards. However, in the longer term it might be expected to result primarily in uncertainty, and may impede the identification and attainment of regulatory goals.

The issues raised for the public lawyer in the context of media regulation are both widespread and obvious. Extending beyond the intricacies of individual court decisions in judicial review cases involving regulatory bodies, the network of, often interrelating and overlapping regulatory institutions and the role of government in relation to them, and, the existence of both statutory and non-statutory regimes all provide obvious focal points.

We can also readily identify problems arising out of the different approaches which are likely to be adopted by national and international bodies which may approach issues from different jurisprudential, constitutional and economic perspectives. It is therefore surprising to find that while adequate legal commentaries are readily available, surprisingly little analysis has been carried out by public lawyers, in the UK at least. There are honourable exceptions to this: in the past, Norman D. Lewis and Mike Elliott have identified and focused upon aspects of this agenda, and Tom Gibbons has taken the time and trouble to pursue a more wide-ranging analysis, though this work has now been largely overtaken by events.

Recently, Lesley Hitchens has made a significant contribution in scrutinising recent developments and indicating the need for a more thorough and considered policy review. However, the net effect of these contributions, while enlightening in many ways, is to leave largely untouched the underlying issues, focusing as they do primarily upon specific developments and occurrences rather than the broader issues and rationales which underlie the subject.

Rather like the activities of government and the media regulators, the focus of commentators has tended to be on amendments to the institutional structure and the outcomes of regulation and its reform rather than upon the rationales for the regulatory endeavour.Such tinkering with the fine detail is unlikely to equip us adequately to address the challenges posed by the ongoing media revolution. It seems largely futile to examine regulatory policies, mechanisms and outcomes without first reflecting upon the objectives deriving from principles, in turn born of the rationales for intervention.

The range of rationales in play suggest a significant role for the media specialist, the political scientist, economist, sociologist and many others, but the lawyer, arguably, must justify their interest. Conventional British legal academics have done little more than to catalogue or chronicle the legal rules in play, however, a wider view of law can be applied. While public lawyers clearly have an interest in the administrative law and practice applicable to an area such as media regulation, they must also place this in its constitutional context, and scrutinise legitimacy and rationality as well as mere legality. Such an approach demands not only the examination of technical rules, but also their relationship to fundamental constitutional and democratic values.

A conventional public law analysis of the institutions of media regulation can offer much, both in terms of substantive and procedural comment. However, there is a sense in which such critique becomes vacuous if not integrated with an understanding of the values which inform any such regime. At the heart of liberal-democratic theory is a concept of citizenship. If citizenship implies effective participation in society, it can be argued that in an era where effective participation has come to rely increasingly upon access to the media as the primary arena for political and cultural communication, access to the media has itself become a prerequisite of effective citizenship.

'Access', in this context, clearly implies the ability to receive media output, but also, arguably, implies an ability to input to the media and influence the agenda. Even if the focus is predominantly on access to the media in terms of receiving media output, the public lawyer, in addition to considering the nature of rules and norms existing in this field, and the quality of the administrative process, must also recognise that access to the media should be utilised as a yardstick when examining existing and proposed regulatory mechanisms.

In the absence of adequate clarity regarding the rationales and objectives of regulation, it is unlikely that we can analyse meaningfully the policies, mechanisms and results of regulation. Therefore, we must step back from the intricacies and specifics of institutional design and focus instead upon the justifications, principles and goals of media regulation.

Objectives

A potentially bewildering array of regulatory techniques have grown up in Britain and comparable jurisdictions, ranging from statutory to self-regulatory methods, and based at both national and international levels. These various approaches can be divided further into general and media-specific competition measures, and those focused on form (or structure of ownership) and effects (or behaviour and its consequences) within media markets. Specific regulatory frameworks may exist not only in relation to ownership and licensing of broadcasting or print-media corporations, but also in relation to content or output. Increasingly, regulatory attention must turn also to delivery mechanisms, and CASs and the like. Often, specific techniques have been developed in relation to particular sectors of the media, but modern developments require a global view on a cross-media basis cutting across conventional sectoral divides.

Acknowledgement of the convergence of telecommunications and broadcasting media can be seen to be implicitly acknowledged in the overlapping roles of the ITC and Oftel in relation to licensing and regulation of the CAS arrangements for DTT, yet this must be viewed simply as one more incremental change, rather than the radical overhaul of the regulatory regime that is indicated.

Marsden suggests that regulation for competition between platforms (DTT, direct-to-home (DTH) satellite, and cable) must be the key for telecommunications liberalisation. Though delivery of television by cable in Britain remains far below the levels achieved in mainland Europe, DTH satellite broadcasting provides an obvious source of competition to DTT, though is itself dominated by BSkyB.

Ensuring the existence of a range of platforms would, however, require a high degree of structural regulation, and arguably a degree of intervention which no British government would be likely to support. Indeed, though committed to the activities of market forces in relation to the media, preferring largely, for example, to allow an industry standard for CASs to emerge rather than imposing one, all government (both Conservative and Labour) rhetoric and legislative activity in the last two years has supported the development of DTT, for example by seeking to ensure quality and attractiveness of product by guaranteeing space on the multiplexes for the conventional, terrestrial, public service broadcasters.

In so far as a common thread can be discerned running through the regulatory arrangements, this thread can be identified as market-oriented. In Britain, and other countries in which current perceptions of democracy tend to push governments away from direct intervention in media output, regulation of ownership, in the name of market competition, has become a significant means of seeking to achieve desired outcomes.

General competition law provisions provide the background here though differences in emphasis between different regimes should be noted. In Britain, investigations into mergers and take-overs will normally be triggered by the acquisition taking a holding beyond a stated limit within a market (form-based competition regulation) while within the EU, the emphasis is on effects rather than form, based on the provisions of Articles 85 and 86 which seek to prohibit restriction or distortion of competition or abuse of a dominant position within a market.

However, in addition to general competition law provisions, media specific measures seek to establish limits on ownership and control of enterprises either within or across media sectors. These range from the provisions of the Fair Trading Act 1973, which allows wide discretion to the Secretary of State in regulating control of newspaper take-overs and mergers, to the complex provisions on cross-media ownership contained in the Broadcasting Act 1996. The overall objective here would appear to be diversity of output, though the regulatory focus is clearly on ownership.

There is a real sense in which the focus on competition via control of ownership can be viewed as surrogate for regulation for plurality in output. This option is obviously tempting given that, though by no means easy, and subject to varying methods of calculation, it is somewhat easier to measure and impose limits on ownership than to determine and define requirements of diversity in output. However, the emphasis on competition law, both general and media-specific measures, as the primary mechanism of ensuring plurality in the media can be questioned, a number of commentators having identified the underlying problem.

According to Humphreys one of the main challenges for the future will be to keep the media diverse and pluralistic in the face of powerful pressures towards economic concentration'. Meanwhile, Beltrame correctly identifies the extent to which competition law can be seen as too blunt an instrument to ensure the desired diversity of output, noting that the European Commission 'argues that the objectives of competition law and those of media ownership laws are profoundly different, in that mergers which, economically speaking do not threaten competition, might well suffocate plurality of media'. Expressing a similar point, slightly more directly, Collins and Murroni note that, 'In spite of technological change, media and communication markets do not fit the paradigms on which competition law is built'. This raises a concept to which we will return, namely, that the media, by virtue of their power and influence, cannot be treated simply as another commodity market, but that the recipients of media products have expectations not only as consumers, but also as citizens.

The fact that the media supplies and influences our view of the world, and has become the primary means for civic, political and cultural communication, demands a degree of equality of access to the media's output if equality of citizenship is acknowledged as a legitimate objective.However, it is the perceived benefits of market competition that underlie the basic framework of competition law, and also drove the British government to take a passive attitude towards the development of CAS equipment, preferring to allow a market driven standard to emerge. European moves towards regulation via structural separation of programming from carriage are premised on consumer benefit which will arise from markets being liberalised and gateways kept open or opened. However, Harcourt notes that despite repeated pressure from the European Parliament, moves towards EU measures on media concentration have been delayed by the nature of the institutional dynamics within and between the Directorates General of the Commission, and political tensions between Member States, indicating the risk of institutional inertia arising in the absence of an appropriate regulatory framework being established.

Regulatory Traditions

Marsden also correctly draws attention to the problems raised for regulators operating within different regulatory traditions. In liberalised and privatised telecommunications markets such as

Britain, telecommunications have largely been regulated by reference to behavioural standards, while regulation of television has largely continued to be carried out on a structural basis, the emphasis being very much on ownership, though with the addition of industry-specific behavioural controls in the form of regulation of content.

Where regulators operating from different traditions are called to act together, tensions will be inevitable. Marsden seems to indicate the likelihood of the 'turf war' between the ITC and Oftel over regulation of CASs being decided in Oftel's favour, with the resulting probability of behavioural regulation predominating. This, it can be argued, would be fundamentally unsatisfactory, at least if behavioural regulation became the predominant or single track approach.

Ultimately, behavioural regulation in relation to specific pinch-points addresses directly the perceived problems of competition within the market, but, such regulation cannot operate effectively alone. It depends for its effectiveness upon the existence of a genuinely competitive market environment beyond specific bottlenecks which in itself, arguably, requires structural regulation.

Anti-competitive behaviour at particular pinch-points will be influenced and shaped by pressures arising from activities in the broader field, and attempts to regulate behaviour, say, in relation to CASs for DTT, will be doomed to failure if the entire environment in which DTT operates is ultimately shaped by the structure of the broader media industry beyond the DTT marketplace. This is the very structural problem which Oftel correctly identifies as problematic in its advice to the ITC regarding DTT multiplex licence allocation.

All this appears to take us down a road towards suggesting a unified scheme of regulation for broadcasting and telecommunications though probably, logically, in light of the increasingly international nature of media holdings, one with a significant international focus. Such an institutional structure must draw on aspects of both structural and behavioural regulation (considering both the corporate structure of media conglomerates and their share of markets, but also, how dominant positions are actually used in relation to competition) but before it can carry out such a task effectively, meaningful objectives must be determined from more clearly articulated rationales for intervention.

In part, any mismatch between regulatory mechanisms and outcomes on the one hand and regulatory values and objectives on the other may be explained by virtue of the clear inconsistencies and conflicts discernible both within and between the various justifications for media regulation. In particular, the conflict between economies of scale, and perceived national interests in the development of large domestic media corporations must be set against the claimed benefits of pluralism and diversity.

The failure to develop a rational basis for the resolution of this conflict may be considered to be the most obvious cause of inconsistent and unsatisfactory regulation under existing and past arrangements. However, it can be argued that the greater degree of lack of achievement in regulation arises simply out of inadequate consideration of the fundamental, underlying values. Such lack of reflection on fundamentals, and the failure to articulate objectives with reasonable clarity goes some way towards explaining the generally reactive nature of regulatory change noted by Elliott over fifteen years ago.

The apparent objectives of regulation vary between prevention of monopoly (or abuse of monopolistic/monopsonistic/oligopolistic power), the protection of differing versions of 'public service' values, and the provision of choice, in terms of product, political viewpoint, and cultural diversity.

Arguably, the debate over objectives has increasingly been

focused on consumer choice of media product, at the expense of broader, citizen oriented, expectations such as those underlying the public service tradition in broadcasting or the imposition of Universal Service Obligations (USOs) in relation to utilities.

Emphasising consumer choice, apparently as an end in itself, avoids the establishment of policy preferences in terms of specific, substantive outcomes or objectives. This produces not only an undue emphasis on (a version of) one rationale for regulatory intervention, but also, by allowing consumer choice to determine the ultimate shape of the media market, creates a high degree of uncertainty. For example, it is unclear whether, in an open market, the consumer would ultimately be tempted most by the charms of DTT, or satellite services, or broad-band cable facilities. Traders in each will be plying their wares, but ultimately this may result in an undesirable trade war, replicating in a new forum the kind of battle of formats between VHS and Betamax in the home video market which resulted in so much consumer dissatisfaction before VHS finally won-out.

The address to the Royal Television Society in September 1997 by Chris Smith, Secretary of State for Culture, Media and Sport confirmed that the present government is following the lead of its predecessor, in facilitating the development of DTT. However, it is by no means certain that this is what the consumer market would or will prefer. If serious about the creation of market choice, a government may find itself with no logical alternative to regulating for a range of acceptable, alternative delivery platforms though even this must be carried out in such a way as to integrate the regulation of control of platforms alongside transmission, production and CASs as part of the broadcasting market as a whole.

It is probably correct for the regulatory emphasis to shift increasingly towards delivery mechanisms, however, when focusing on this particular area, the regime must remain aware of the broader market context in which delivery mechanisms exist, and be informed by clear objectives, arising out of clearly defined rationales for intervention. To intervene is not to deny market forces, but to give effect to them. Almost nowhere does a market survive which is not regulated, and in an area such as the media, which shows such clear tendencies towards monopoly, regulation is the necessary partner of market forces if the perceived benefits of the market are to accrue.

Regulatory Rationales: Different Approaches

Ultimately, a consistent and effective regime of regulation can only exist where the justification for regulation is articulated with reasonable clarity, and in this respect difficult choices must be made between competing and often conflicting rationales. It is this area of the debate where failure to date has been the greatest.

Justifications for regulating the media can, broadly, be broken-down into three or four groups.

The first relates to effectiveness of communication. In the context of the broadcast media, a particular related version of this argument has been that effective broadcast communication of necessity required regulation of broadcasting, as a result of the need to allocate and separate frequencies to avoid intermodulation (cross-channel interference). While of some strength historically, this argument is about to lose all currency in the context of the vast, almost infinite, expansion of channels available as a result of digital and satellite technology.

The second group of arguments for regulating the media derive from arguments which can, again, be broadly classified as pluralist. Thus, arising from an acknowledgement of the power of the media, we find, in the liberal-democratic context, arguments for diversity of ownership, with the aim of ensuring the circulation of a range of views: cultural and political diversity. On occasion, such arguments can be amended significantly to provide a cultural-protectionist version. The protection of minority languages such as Dutch, or even major languages such as French, against the cultural imperialism of a (US) English dominated world media can be conceived as an argument for cultural and linguistic diversity on the global scale.

These first two rationales for regulation seem to derive from rationales for freedom of expression based on arguments from truth, self-fulfilment or citizen participation though both are clearly premised on the perceived liberal-democratic ideal of the ability of all to have access to the 'market-place of ideas'.

Running parallel to this is a third, economics based, argument, that monopoly, and even possibly oligopoly, is undesirable as it denies the perceived benefits that are said to derive from the operation of an effective market.

Deriving from the second argument's concern with plurality of media material, and potentially cutting across the third of avoidance of monopoly, is a fourth line of argument. This concerns a public service ethos, which though encapsulated in Britain by Reith's tripartite typology of 'informing, educating and entertaining' will be interpreted differently in different countries.

While regulation with a sole objective of preserving public service values may inhibit market developments, and may indeed ultimately stifle plurality of media product, the public service rationale for media regulation is said to derive from a desire to ensure the availability of a range of quality products, especially in relation to the media's role of enhancing the viewer's or reader's view of the world.

The public service approach is related to the 'social responsibility' model identified by Siebert et al, acknowledging the crucial role played by the media in equipping individual citizens for participation in society, while also acknowledging that the media is hugely significant in terms of providing 'a cultural cohesion to the nation'.

All of these various rationales for regulating the media must be considered when regulatory reform is broached. It is only rarely, however, that the competing rationales can be or will be neatly separated. Rather, they will often be melded together and encapsulated in what can prove to be a singularly unhelpful term: 'the public interest'. Whenever this term appears it requires the closest possible scrutiny, as it invariably comprises a portmanteau, the contents of which must be examined closely. Sometimes, it will contain a meaning approximating to one of the rationales set-out above, sometimes more than one, sometimes all four in some combination.

In UK, under the terms of Paragraphs 9-13 of Schedule 2 to the Broadcasting Act 1996, the ITC and the Radio Authority are charged with applying a test of public interest when considering the acquisition of commercial broadcasting licences by cross-media corporations already controlling one or more newspapers. The criteria to be applied as indicative of the public interest as set-out in Paragraph 13, include:

a) the desirability of promoting:

    i) plurality of ownership in the broadcasting and newspaper industries, and

    ii) diversity in the sources of information available to the public and in the opinions expressed on television or radio or in newspapers,

b) any economic benefits

c) the effect of the holding of the licence by that body on the proper operation of the market within the broadcasting and newspaper industries or any section of them.

The tension and conflict between these competing public interest claims is obvious. The regulators will have to balance potential economic benefits against the values of plurality and diversity and the effects on competition. This leaves the regulators with an unenviable task, akin to comparing apples with oranges, and, in the British context, we cannot be sure that any such decision will be taken via a transparent process, or even that adequate reasons will be given or required to enable us to check the rationality of such decision-making. Thus, the absence of a meaningful construct of 'public interest' not only permits, if not encourages, inconsistency in regulation, but also hands to regulators significant, and largely unchecked, discretionary power.

Underlying various rationales for regulation are differing versions of arguments relating to freedom of effective expression, dependant increasingly upon access to the media. The approaches adopted often take on board arguments relating to diversity in media products, both in political and cultural terms, but will also often be influenced also by economic, market-driven arguments, and may also seek to perpetuate public service values.

It is argued that all of these approaches are, within the context of liberal-democracies, premised upon expectations of citizenship, and that effective access to the media is in effect a prerequisite of effective citizenship. With this in mind, to place citizenship at the heart of any meaningful concept of 'the public interest' would seem to be a logical necessity. The move away from a world of five analogue, terrestrial television channels to a new era of interactive television integrated with wider computer and telecommunications facilities, accessible in many cases via costly gateway facilities, presents the risk of heightened social division; an increase in the hierarchy of information 'haves' and 'have nots' and therefore heightened social inequality.

Whether the media revolution will result in the end of mass-media, with fragmentation along the lines of electronic publishing resulting, or monopoly by dominant programme or delivery mechanism suppliers. At least in the medium term, it is possible to envisage elements of both co-existing. A degree of cultural fragmentation can be expected when not everyone will have watched the same sport or soap, or surfed the same site the night before; when not everyone will have had access to the same range of options. The 'cultural cohesion' will inevitably be challenged. At the same time, however, the market may be dominated through control of transmission or gateway facilities by one or two major players, be those people Rupert Murdoch, Bill Gates, or whoever, who may be seen as exercising undue influence over the available range of products. The latter phenomenon may result in a high degree of homogeneity of product and a very limited degree of plurality of political standpoints.

Either of these outcomes might intuitively be considered undesirable, but some such outcome seems inevitable if active regulation is not undertaken quickly. Limits on sectoral or even cross-media ownership seem to have limited effects, unless adequate regulatory attention is paid to key bottlenecks or pinch-points. Likewise, no matter how effective regulatory action ensuring free-flow through these bottlenecks is, the range of media products flowing through may be limited if the production and distribution process is subjected to an undue degree of domination.

At the most general level, Collins and Murroni state that 'What is needed is competition policy where competition can thrive in the public interest and regulation where it cannot'. In itself, this seems perfectly reasonable, though ultimately is heavily dependant upon an adequately developed and transparent concept of 'the public interest'. While this analysis indicates clearly the need for regulation based on both structural and behavioural foundations, such a prescription may do more harm than good if it stifles innovation and/or has an adverse impact on economic development. For this prescription to provide positive outcomes, it must be applied as part of a broader regime of treatment, but focused on identified goals derived from rational, public and widespread and informed debate.

Despite emphasising the necessity of viewing the media increasingly on a global basis, and the growing presence in this field of regional organisations such as the EU, Herman and McChesney note that 'nation states remain the most important political forces in communication and much else'. Thus, national responses to global phenomena must still be determined.

The classical arena for such discourse in a liberal-democracy such as Britain is via the conventional political channels, however, in an age in which the zeitgeist appears to demand liberalisation or de-regulation, it may prove difficult to persuade politicians to grasp this regulatory nettle.

In an era in which market-based philosophy enjoys a virtually unchallenged hegemonic position, it is difficult for a government to take so unfashionable a position as to limit the influence of market forces by reference to other, arguably higher, values. However, for a government said to value citizenship and community, taking steps to ensure social inclusion and equality of citizenship would be perfectly consistent. In a sense, therefore, unfashionably, Collins and Murroni advocate the active exercise of policy-making power, and also regulatory power, in the public interest. This active, policy-making role is unfashionable in the sense that hands-off government, and liberalisation or de-regulation, is the dominant philosophy in British politics, exemplifying the hegemonic success of Thatcherite 'philosophy'.

However, we only have to consider the present state of confusion over media regulation, the failure of regulation in Italy and Britain to control the rise to dominance of Berlusconi and Murdoch respectively, and the reactive, ill-considered nature of policy-making in this area identified by Hitchens, to realise that Humphreys is correct in noting that 'liberalising re-regulation' is unlikely to provide an adequate response.

The major problem is the identification and articulation of regulatory objectives, often masked by the use of the nebulous 'public interest'. The common thread underlying the public interest claims in relation to media regulation can best be described as feeding into the broader constitutional endeavour of effective citizen participation.

Effective participation can be equated with informed participation, and this in turn requires a diverse range of views to be in circulation and accessible to as wide a range of the population as possible in order to allow for comparison and triangulation.

Concentration in media markets, though not necessarily contrary to diversity of content, tends to have a strong contingent effect of limiting the range of views available for scrutiny. This effect can already be readily observed in the British newspaper sector, and now, with increasing dependence upon new technology to access broadcast information and computer information resources, both at a price, concentration presents a dual threat of risking further concentration in relation to technological gateways and simultaneously creating a two-tier information society. However, inadequately considered responses will not help, and revisions of regulatory structures and techniques without adequately addressing the fundamental underlying value-questions, will not help either.

A possible, and potentially attractive, way forward is offered by Collins and Murroni, who, in presenting their analysis of the challenges currently facing media regulation, draw upon the findings of the IPPR's Commission on Social Justice. The Commission established four objectives which it believed should influence government policy:

— *'security'* : policies aimed at prevention, or failing that relief, of poverty;

— *'opportunity'* : policies designed 'to increase autonomy and life chances';

— *'democracy'* : 'policies designed to ensure diffusion of power within government and between government and people';

— *'fairness'*: 'policies designed to reduce unjustified inequality' (or social exclusion).

The Commission seeks to apply these as 'Benchmarks through which policy makers as well as the public can judge policy options'.The last three of these, may also serve equally well as criteria against which the effectiveness of the activities of media regulators may be measured. Outcomes of regulation can be assessed against these standards.

To date, we have had reactive regulation, focusing on form within the sectoral and cross-media marketplaces and largely consisting of ex post facto reaction to changing technological circumstances. Now, and in the future, positive regulation will be required to ensure the widespread circulation of and access to a range of information and cultural products, and this must be positively confirmed as the key regulatory objective. Something akin to USOs may need to be imposed, but, in terms of regulatory practice, integrated regulation of the cross-media market, including control of technological gateways, focused on outcomes is necessary if this objective is to be achieved.

Regulation of ownership in conventional media markets has often been employed as what can be viewed as a surrogate for regulating for diversity of product. In the modern context, however, attention must also be paid to regulating control of delivery mechanisms. It may be that only by regulating for the existence of a range of delivery platforms can meaningful diversity be created, or, in so far as it presently exists, be maintained.

Regulation for common-carriage, as advocated by Humphreys, or 'must carry' requirements, also has its attractions, a form of imposing USOs on those who control delivery mechanisms. However, even this must be coupled with regulation of ownership to avoid domination of distribution and production. The resulting complex congeries of regulatory targets will inevitably result in a confusing, and potentially contradictory regulatory framework if the underlying rationale(s) for regulation are not adequately spelled-out.

Future of the Mass Audience

Despite the advanced technology, the audience of the future will take one of two directions. Depending on the funding of the new media, audiences will either be small and insignificant, or audiences will be controlled by corporate forces.

The future of the mass audience lies in between complete government control and an active pluralist democracy. With the rise of new technologies that will allow a more horizontal, user-controlled media, the structure of society will be altered. Due to post-industrialism, which created separations within the community, people have sought a sense of belonging. With the rise of new media technology, people will be vulnerable to media control. This idea is contrasted with the belief that new media will be easily accessible and allow users to be educated. The audience will actively participate in a type of "town hall" marketplace of ideas, which is indicative of a true democracy. However, the push of technology will be countered by two forces.

The onset of new media technology will be opposed by two forces. One involves the behavior of the mass communications audience. Throughout the communications revolution, media has not captured the attention of its active audience. Rather, the audience selectively participates in media. The force of the technological communications revolution will be significantly constrained by the partial attentiveness and limited energies of the mass audience.

The second force involves the political economy of the American mass communications industry. The privately owned media demands profits. Because of this, the content of the new media will not differ greatly from traditional forms of media.

There are many advantages to the new media, among which are decreasing costs, increasing extensibility, increasing volume, increasing channel diversity, and increasing interconnectivity. What Neuman neglected to mention was the cost that these advances will entail. He first discusses decreasing costs. True, the costs of media technology are decreasing due to technological advances.

However, the past has proved that technology moves so rapidly that the equipment is continually being replaced by more advanced and more expensive forms. It is an endless cycle of the past's equipment being replaced by today's equipment, which gets replaced by tomorrow's equipment. Costs do decrease, but by this time the consumer runs the risk of his purchase being outdated by newer technology. This cycle is evident in computer, stereo, and video technology. This argument is countered by the increasing extensibility of technology. However, software is not immune from the cycles of technology and costs either.

As newer and more advanced software is developed, existing software will become outdated. Thus, the cycle continues. Increasing volume, channel diversity, and interconnectivity will all cost money. Finding information takes time and effort, and it will cost money to search databases such as Nexis. New, diverse channels of communication must be purchased, much like cable television. The interconnectivity that allows traditional forms of media to be accessed through one medium does not mean that it will cost any less. Movies, magazines, and music must still be purchased. Due to the many costs of new media, the future of the mass audience will head in one of two directions.

The key to controlling the content of the media is to look at who pays for it. There are two ways that the new media will be funded: either by the consumers or by advertisers. Both funding methods are utilized within existing media communications. Government funding is unlikely due to past precedent. Historically the government has left media in the private sector and plays a very limited role within media. However, whichever way the new media is funded, the result will be different from what Neuman predicts.

If the consumer funds the use of the new media technologies, a situation much like public television will be created. The new media will be viewer or audience-funded and depending on the medium, may only be available to those willing to pay. This will result in a limited audience who has spent a lot of money to utilize the technology. The content of information may be much more diverse and desirable to the audience than currently exists in traditional media. However, the amount of people who have access to it will be insignificant due to costs. In addition to the technological equipment costs, a unique situation may arise concerning the nature of information.

Whereas television is cost-free to the consumer, this new media will not be. Thus, information becomes a commodity that must be purchased by the user. It will be similar to pay-per-view television in that one must pay for individual programs. Thus, if the user desires certain content, he will have to pay for it. The existence of a pluralist democracy may develop, but only within this small, elite group that has access to the media.

The limited effects of new media communications will be due more to the high access cost. The Internet computer system, which gives users access to a wealth of information, is indicative of this new media. In order to use it, users must have access to a computer, a phone line, and own an account, all of which require money. For this reason, only a small percentage of the population has access to the Internet. It has been heralded as the electronic "town hall," but currently it is a very small and limited democracy. Consumer funding is the only way to guarantee content diversity, but the lack of an audience may result in a search for other funding for new media. The other direction that new media may take is towards corporate funding.

Corporate and advertiser funding of new media communications will allow the audience free access to the information, but this will result in homogeneous media content and subtler forms of media control. Television is an example of a corporate and advertiser funded medium. Neuman discussed the corporate structure of the media, which will hold true for this new media. Success is measured by audience size, and in order to achieve this media must appeal to mainstream interests. Despite technological advances within communications equipment, the content will remain as homogeneous as always. Corporate control, as well as advertising control, will be just as prevalent with the new media as it is with traditional media.

Traditionally in media, there is a distinct line between ads and actual content. New media will result in a blurring of the distinction between advertising and information. This trend can be viewed in the traditional media form of television, as infomercials, which are advertising-funded programs, become prevalent. In new computer-based media, this trend will permeate the content of information. Because they are aware that users will only access desired information, advertisers will rely on this information to sell their products. There will be information about advertisers' products, as well as advertiser-sponsored information.

The Internet's World Wide Web has many examples of this. Businesses have "home pages" where users can obtain information about their product. For example, Warner Brothers has a "home page" that has information about their music artists, movies, and magazines. Other corporations will choose to provide non-product related information, as long as the user knows who is sponsoring it. Miller Genuine Draft sponsors a page that lists popular restaurants in various cities across the country. Corporations will try to disguise their advertisements as information, which will result in corporate control of the audience. Perhaps this approach will be more successful for advertisers, because the economic influence is subtler and less obvious to the consumer. As opposed to propaganda, which blasts the message to the audience, this blurring of information and advertising may confuse users. What could result is corporate control. Though the audience believes they are in control, because they cannot discern ads from information, they are not.

The new media will not be under the control of government or corporations. Rather, the audience will control it. However, media technology is not free. Costs will be high and someone will have to pay for it. If the trend is towards consumer-funded media, control will be in the hands of the people, which Neuman believes will happen. Unfortunately, the access to it will be expensive and in small demand. This may work for a time, but much like Warner Communication's QUBE, the new media may not have enough participation to make a difference. If funding is corporate-based, the future may be even less optimistic.